To my fabulous parents, Astrida and Alex Reader.
You have shown me, through love, encouragement, kindness
and determination, that anything is possible. Celebrating your
50th wedding anniversary—in June 2002—you are now,
as then, passionately in love.
Congratulations!

Teddy

Contents

Acknowledgments

To my family and friends, who endured hours of tastings, consumption and patience. Cheers, and thanks. And much thanks to:

The crew of King of the Q Television Inc.: Kirk, Craig, Joe, Leslie and all the gang.

Jessica Reader: for all your help.

Uni Foods and Steven Mintz: one of my biggest supporters.

Celtrade Canada and Ron McAvan: thanks for the daily chat and for being a great guy.

The folks at M&M Meat Shops: hundreds of meal ideas and only one aisle!

Jack Daniel's: mmmmm, delicious.

Maple Lodge Farms: they do chicken right.

Spice Islands: the spice of life, and of my cooking.

Heritage Salmon: because Atlantic salmon from Heritage doesn't get any better.

Per Kristensen Photography: for making it all look so beautiful and delicious.

Introduction

I recently took delivery of an authentic tandoori oven from northern India. Simply constructed and made of special clay, the tandoori oven burns hard wood, which adds a wonderful aroma to whatever you cook in it. It's also one of the hottest cooking methods going. Meat, fish and fowl are placed on skewers and put into the oven, where the searing heat traps the spices and natural juices of the food. The food comes out cooked on the outside, moist and tender on the inside and bursting with flavor.

My tandoori oven is a perfect addition to the collection of barbecues and outdoor grills that now takes up most of my garage and backyard patio. (Thankfully, Pamela puts up with my obsession and is always the first to enjoy the food these grills produce—with my help, of course!) My assortment of outdoor cookers includes my old faithful charcoal kettle, a combo gas-fired charcoal grill and a number of propane grills.

My friends joke that I have so many barbecues that if I arranged them on a stage like a drum kit I could hold nightly performances for anyone with half an appetite. They make light of my collection and my trademark showmanship, but what they don't realize is that barbecuing is more than cooking—it's a performance art. And like any artist, I take my inspiration from a wide variety of sources—people I meet, restaurants I enjoy, things I read and places I visit.

In my capacity as a food consultant, writer and television chef, I do a lot of traveling. When I was in India, I enjoyed an absolutely outstanding meal of traditional tandoori food, an experience that prompted me to buy my tandoori oven. Recalling my trip to India got me thinking about all the other fascinating encounters I've been lucky enough to enjoy over the years and how important they've been in igniting my passion for grilling. Once I started compiling all these juicy tidbits from all over, I realized that I had more than enough inspiration to create a sequel to my previous bestselling cookbook, *Sticky Fingers and Tenderloins*. The result is this book.

The theme of this cookbook is grillin' and lovin' it. Like good loving, good grilling requires creativity and imagination. I've used my culinary adventures and travels to create Kama Sutra Cinnamon-Skewered Chicken Thighs, Miami Spice Love Paste, Grilled Chicken Breasts Stuffed with Peaches, Brie and Shrimp, Sticky Love Chops, Grilled Venison Rack Chops with Smoked Chocolate and Poblano Chili Sauce, Mashed Sweet Potatoes with Marshmallow Butter and on and on.

"Cauldrons from the Hearth" features delicious soups, like Denver Hamburger Soup, which I picked up from a flight attendant from Colorado, and Creamy Smoked Garlic and Cheddar Chowder—a garlic taste to die for!

After you down some "Sexy Salads," enjoy my "Finger-Licking Sandwiches." Try my Hoser HAM-burger. Tastes great with beer!

From the sea, I've reeled in wonderfully wet and wild recipes such as Grilled Jumbo Frogs' Legs, Cedar-Planked Salmon with Crab and Scallop Crust, and Grilled Calamari with Balsamic Butter Sauce. You also have to try out some—or all!—of the chicken and meat recipes in the chapters "Hot-Buttered Breasts and Thighs" and "Lip-Smacking Tenderloins." They're all outstanding! For steak lovers, there's the Big Man's 2002 Porterhouse Steak with Dijon Cream Sauce. I'm a big guy and I'm dedicating this steak recipe to moi!

As many of you already know, ribs are my specialty. Try the Guinness-Braised Baby Back Ribs with Sweet Molasses BBQ Sauce or the Chili Pineapple Baby Back Ribs. They're all rib-o-licious, baby!

You'll also find liquid libations such as Chocolate Banana Rum Milkshakes; luxurious appetizers including Cedar-Planked Brie with Oyster Mushroom and Roasted Garlic Crust; and drooling desserts such as Grilled Bacon-Wrapped Bananas with Bourbon Honey Sauce. Yummy!

Throughout the book I use a unique method of calculating grilling time. I call it the Beerometer, and it equates grill time with volume of beer consumed. In other words, if a recipe takes 15 to 20 minutes to grill, for most guys (and gals) that would be the same time as it takes to consume one beer.

Here's a handy reference:

Time	Beerometer
5 to 15 minutes	1 Beer
15 to 30 minutes	2 Beers
30 to 45 minutes	3 Beers
45 to 60 minutes	4 Beers

You get the drift.

Given some of the taste combinations I've devised for this book, you'll agree that I'm pushing the barbecue envelope to the limit. But why not? I believe that when it comes to food, there are no rules. When grilling, the goal is to have as much fun as possible and to turn each meal into your own personalized work of art. So get out there and perform!

As for my new tandoori oven, I'm sure it will provide great new taste sensations and hours of fun and entertainment for my family and friends. I already feel another cookbook coming on! *Ted's Tandoori*, anyone?

Cauldrons from the Hearth

Denver Hamburger Soup

On a recent flight to Denver, I had the pleasure of chatting with a flight attendant named Sherry. She gave me the recipe for this hearty, warming soup. Thanks, Sherry—it's not only original but also delicious.

1/2 cup	butter		1 tsp.	salt
1	large onion, diced		1 tsp.	ground black pepper
4 cloves	garlic, minced		1/4 cup	vegetable oil
2 stalks	celery, diced		1 tbsp.	Worcestershire sauce
2	carrots, diced		1 tsp.	hot sauce
2	large potatoes, peeled and diced			Salt and pepper to taste
1/2 cup	all-purpose flour		**Garnishes**	
10 cups	beef stock or broth		2 cups	shredded Cheddar cheese
2 lb.	regular ground beef or turkey		1/2 cup	bacon bits
1 tbsp.	dried oregano		1/2 cup	sour cream
1 tsp.	ground cumin		2	green onions, finely chopped
1 tsp.	chili powder			

1. In a large soup pot, melt the butter over medium-high heat. Add the onion, garlic, celery, carrots and potatoes; sauté until the onions are transparent, 4 to 5 minutes.
2. Stir in the flour; cook, stirring constantly, for 2 minutes. Add the beef stock in stages, stirring until fully incorporated. Bring to a boil, reduce heat and simmer for 30 minutes, stirring frequently to prevent sticking.
3. Meanwhile, in a large bowl, mix the ground beef, oregano, cumin, chili, salt and pepper.
4. Heat the oil in a large frying pan over medium-high heat. Sauté the beef until fully cooked. Using a slotted spoon, transfer the ground beef to the soup. Season with Worcestershire sauce, hot sauce, salt and pepper. Simmer for another 15 minutes.
5. Serve in warmed soup crocks garnished with Cheddar cheese, bacon bits, sour cream and green onions. Serve with lightly buttered toasted hamburger buns.

Serves 8 to 10

Grilled Summer Vegetable Soup

The first year in our new home, Pamela and I decided to plant a vegetable garden. This is a recipe that we created using some of our backyard produce.

1/4 cup + 2 tbsp.	olive oil	2 ears	corn, shucked
			Salt and pepper to taste
1/4 cup	apple cider vinegar	4 cloves	garlic, minced
1	large onion, quartered	1	very small habanero pepper, seeded and finely chopped
1	large leek, cut in half lengthwise and washed of all grit	2 stalks	celery, sliced
1	zucchini, cut in half lengthwise	2	large Yukon Gold potatoes, peeled and diced
1	large bulb fennel, cut in half lengthwise	8 cups	vegetable or chicken stock
2	red bell peppers, cut in half lengthwise	1 lb.	green or scarlet runner beans, cut into 1-inch pieces
8	plum tomatoes	1 tbsp.	chopped fresh thyme
		1 tbsp.	chopped fresh basil

1. Preheat grill to medium-high.
2. In a large bowl, whisk together 1/4 cup of the olive oil and the vinegar. Add the onion, leek, zucchini, fennel, red peppers, tomatoes, corn, salt and pepper. Toss together well.
3. Grill the vegetables, turning occasionally, until lightly charred and just tender, 10 to 15 minutes. Remove from heat and let cool. Slice all the grilled vegetables into 1-inch pieces and set aside.
4. In a large soup pot, heat the remaining 2 tbsp. of olive oil over medium heat. Add the garlic, habanero and celery; sauté until tender, 3 to 4 minutes. Add the potatoes and stock. Bring to a boil, reduce heat to low and simmer for 10 minutes.
5. Add the sliced grilled vegetables, green beans, thyme and basil. Cook, stirring occasionally, until the potatoes are tender, about 15 minutes. Season to taste with salt and pepper. Serve with grilled crusty bread.

Serves 8 to 10

Creamy Smoked Garlic and Cheddar Chowder

Roasted garlic is one of the hottest culinary trends. It has even been used in ice cream (a little different, but it sure beats smoked salmon ice cream). For this chowder I like to use smoked garlic. It has the same sweetness as roasted but with the added dimension of hickory smoke. If you don't have time to smoke the garlic, substitute roasted garlic.

3 heads	smoked garlic (about 24 cloves) (page 96)	2 cups	heavy cream
4 slices	bacon, diced	1 tbsp.	chopped fresh thyme
1	large onion, diced	1 tbsp.	Worcestershire sauce
1 stalk	celery, diced		Salt and pepper
2	large Yukon Gold potatoes, peeled and diced	2 cups	shredded white Cheddar cheese
1/4 cup	all-purpose flour	2 tbsp.	chopped fresh chives, for garnish
4 cups	vegetable or chicken stock		

1. Peel the smoked garlic cloves and finely chop all the garlic. Set aside.
2. In a large soup pot over medium heat, cook the bacon until just crispy. Using a slotted spoon, remove the bacon and set aside. Add the onion, celery and potatoes to the pot and sauté until the onions are soft, 4 to 5 minutes. Sprinkle in the flour, stirring constantly. Whisk in the stock, one ladle at a time, until fully incorporated. Bring to a boil, stirring.
3. Reduce heat to low. Add the cream, smoked garlic, thyme and Worcestershire sauce. Cover and simmer, stirring occasionally, until potatoes are tender, 15 to 20 minutes.
4. Season to taste with salt and pepper. Stir in Cheddar cheese and reserved bacon. Serve garnished with chives.

Serves 8 to 10

Grilled Chicken, Shrimp and Sausage Gumbo

Visiting New Orleans is a favorite pastime of mine, not only because of all of the great food, partying and music there but because it is truly a culinary mecca. Some of the greatest American chefs have come from New Orleans: Paul Prudhomme, the father of Cajun cuisine; John Folse; and of course Emeril Lagasse.

The key to a great gumbo is the roux. Roux is equal parts of cooked butter or oil and flour. To make a true gumbo, you must first have the patience to prepare a mahogany roux. This requires a bit of time, but all great things take time, and this gumbo just happens to be one of the great culinary creations. A gumbo can consist of virtually anything you want. My favorite is this combination of grilled chicken, andouille sausage and jumbo shrimp.

4	boneless, skinless chicken breasts (each 6 oz.)		1	large onion, diced
1 lb.	extra-large shrimp (16 to 20), peeled and deveined		2 stalks	celery, diced
			12 cups	chicken stock
1/4 cup	Bone Dust BBQ Spice (page 99)		1	large green bell pepper, diced
3/4 cup	vegetable oil		3	green onions, finely chopped
1/2 lb.	andouille or other smoked pork sausage		2 cups	sliced okra
				Louisiana hot sauce
1/2 cup	all-purpose flour			Salt and pepper
4 cloves	garlic, minced			Cooked white rice
1	jalapeño pepper, finely chopped		1/4 cup	chopped fresh parsley, for garnish

1. Preheat grill to medium-high.
2. Coat the chicken and shrimp with Bone Dust BBQ Spice and 1/4 cup of the oil. Grill chicken until fully cooked, 5 to 6 minutes per side; set aside to cool. Grill shrimp until just cooked and opaque, 2 to 3 minutes per side; set aside to cool. Grill sausage until lightly charred and heated through, 4 to 5 minutes per side; set aside to cool.
3. Slice the chicken into 1-inch cubes. Cut each shrimp in half lengthwise. Slice the sausage into 1/4-inch-thick rounds. Set aside chicken, shrimp and sausage.

4. In a large soup pot, heat the remaining $1/2$ cup of vegetable oil over medium-high heat. Add the flour; cook, stirring constantly with a wooden spoon, until roux is golden brown, 2 to 3 minutes, being careful not to burn the roux; if necessary, reduce the heat to medium. If black specks appear in the roux, discard it and start over.
5. Add the garlic, jalapeño, onion and celery. Cook, stirring, until tender, 3 to 5 minutes.
6. Whisk in the stock, one ladle at a time, until fully incorporated. Bring to a boil, stirring. Reduce heat to low. Add the green pepper, green onions and okra. Cover and cook for 20 minutes, stirring occasionally.
7. Fold in grilled chicken, shrimp and sausage. Return to a boil. Season to taste with Louisiana hot sauce, salt and pepper.
8. Place a large spoonful of cooked white rice in each soup bowl and ladle gumbo over rice. Garnish with parsley.

Serves 8 to 10

Smoked Ham and Squash Chowder

This recipe, for convenience, uses store-bought ham. But if you have the time—and a smoker—there is nothing more rewarding than tending your smoker, sucking back a few cold pops and then creating some wonderful meals from a tasty smoked ham.

3 tbsp.	butter	6 cups	chicken stock
1	large onion, diced	3 cups	diced smoked ham
3 cloves	garlic, minced	1 cup	heavy cream
1	jalapeño pepper, seeded and finely chopped	1/4 cup	maple syrup
		2 tbsp.	chopped fresh sage
4 cups	diced butternut squash		Salt and pepper to taste
1 tbsp.	Bone Dust BBQ Spice (page 99)	2 cups	shredded Monterey Jack cheese
1/4 cup	all-purpose flour		

1. In a large soup pot, melt the butter over medium heat. Add the onion, garlic and jalapeño; cook, stirring frequently, until onion is tender, 3 to 4 minutes.
2. Add the squash; cook, stirring frequently, for another 3 to 4 minutes. Add the Bone Dust BBQ Spice and flour, stirring until mixed, about 1 minute.
3. Add the chicken stock, stirring until fully incorporated. Bring to a boil, reduce heat and simmer, uncovered and stirring occasionally, until the squash is soft and the soup is thickened, about 45 minutes. If necessary, add a little more stock to thin the soup.
4. Stir in the ham, cream, maple syrup and sage. Return to a boil, stirring, and cook for 10 minutes. Season with salt and pepper.
5. Serve topped with Monterey Jack cheese.

Serves 8 to 10

Beata's Chilled Sour Dill Pickle Soup

One day my love came home from work with a jar of soup. Her assistant, Beata, had made her family's sour pickle soup. Although a little wary at first, we gave it a try. Beata had said to serve it either hot or cold, so we tried both. My favorite is the chilled version, but Pamela prefers the hot. Use really good pickles for this recipe. Homemade are best, but a really good kosher dill works just as well.

2 tbsp.	olive oil		Garlic Dill Pickles (page 62), grated
1 clove	garlic, minced	1 cup	heavy cream
1	small onion, diced	Pinch	cayenne pepper
1	carrot, diced		Salt and pepper to taste
2	large Yukon Gold potatoes, diced		
1/2 cup	long-grain rice	***Garnishes***	
6 cups	chicken stock		
2 tsp.	Worcestershire sauce	1 cup	sour cream
1 sprig	fresh dill	1 tbsp.	chopped fresh dill
8	sour dill pickles (store-bought) or Spicy	1 tsp.	lemon juice
		1	sour dill pickle, thinly sliced

1. In a large soup pot, heat the oil over medium-high heat. Add the garlic, onion and carrot; sauté until tender, about 3 minutes. Add potatoes and rice; cook, stirring, for 1 minute. Add stock, Worcestershire sauce and dill sprig. Bring to a boil, reduce heat and simmer, uncovered, until the rice and potatoes are fully cooked, 20 to 30 minutes.
2. Add the grated pickles and cream. Return to a boil and simmer until the pickles are tender, about 15 minutes. Season with cayenne, salt and black pepper. Let cool completely. Refrigerate until needed.
3. Just before serving, whisk together the sour cream, dill and lemon juice. Season with salt and pepper.
4. To serve, ladle the soup into chilled bowls and garnish with a dollop of dill sour cream and three thin slices of dill pickle.

Serves 8

Chilled Avocado and Lobster Soup with Habanero Peppers

This soup will refresh you on the hottest of summer days.

2	live lobsters (each about 1¹/₂ lb.)	1	large ripe mango, peeled and diced
¹/₄ cup	olive oil	2	green onions, chopped
2 cloves	garlic, minced	¹/₄ cup	fresh lime juice
1	small habanero pepper, seeded and finely chopped	1 tbsp.	chopped fresh cilantro
1	red onion, diced		Salt and pepper
6 cups	chicken or lobster stock	Pinch	cayenne pepper
3	avocados		Sour cream and fresh cilantro sprigs, for garnish

1. Steam the live lobsters over boiling water for 6 to 8 minutes per pound. Remove from steamer and let cool. (If you do not have a steamer large enough to hold the lobsters, boil them in a large pot of salted water for 6 to 8 minutes per pound.)
2. Crack the lobster shells and remove all of the meat. (Use the shells to prepare lobster stock, if you wish.) Cut the meat into ¹/₄-inch cubes. Cover and refrigerate.
3. In a medium saucepan, heat the oil over medium-high heat. Sauté the garlic, habanero and red onion until tender, 2 to 3 minutes. Add the chicken stock; bring to a rolling boil. Remove from heat and let cool completely.
4. Peel and dice the avocados. Sprinkle with a little lime juice to prevent the avocado from turning brown.
5. In a large bowl, combine the avocado, mango, green onions, lime juice and cilantro. Fold in lobster meat and season to taste with salt and black pepper. Pour in the chilled chicken stock mixture and gently stir until fully mixed. Add the cayenne; adjust seasoning if necessary. Cover and refrigerate for up to 4 hours.
6. To serve, ladle the soup into chilled bowls or mugs and garnish with a dollop of sour cream and a sprig of fresh cilantro.

Serves 6

Wendy's Chipotle Venison Chili with Southern Jalapeño Cornbread

My good friend Wendy is a fabulous chef who used to have a catering company called Babette's Feast. Once, while I was her chef for a year, we made a huge pot of Wendy's amazing Chipotle Venison Chili. Her client was ecstatic with this hot pot of warmth.

3 lb.	venison shoulder, cut into 1-inch cubes	2	poblano peppers, seeded and diced
1	can (7 oz.) chipotle chilies in adobo sauce, puréed	2	red bell peppers, diced
8 cloves	garlic, minced	1 bottle	honey brown lager
1 tbsp.	salt	2	cans (each 14 oz.) diced tomatoes
2 tsp.	black pepper	2 cups	sweet corn kernels (about 4 ears)
2 tsp.	ground coriander	2 tbsp.	chopped fresh cilantro
2 tsp.	ground cumin	3	green onions, finely chopped
2 tsp.	paprika	1	lime, juiced
1/2 cup	all-purpose flour		Sour cream, for garnish
1/2 cup	vegetable oil		Shredded Monterey Jack cheese, for garnish
1	large Spanish onion, diced		
8 slices	thick-cut bacon, cut crosswise into 1/2-inch strips		

1. In a large bowl, season the venison with half of the chipotle chili purée, the garlic, salt, black pepper, coriander, cumin and paprika. Mix well. Marinate, covered and refrigerated, for 24 hours.
2. Sprinkle the flour over the venison and toss to coat. In a large soup pot over medium-high heat, heat the oil. Working in batches if necessary, brown the venison with the onions until the liquid has evaporated and the onions are brown, 10 to 15 minutes. Using a slotted spoon, transfer the venison and onions to a bowl.
3. In the same pot, sauté the bacon until crispy. Drain off excess oil. Return the venison and onions to the pot. Add the remaining chipotle chili purée, the poblano peppers, red peppers, beer and tomatoes with their juice. Bring slowly to a boil over medium

heat, stirring occasionally. Reduce heat to low and cook chili, uncovered and stirring occasionally, for 1 hour or until the venison is extremely tender. Stir in the corn, cilantro, green onions and lime juice. Cook until the corn is tender, about 15 minutes. Season with salt and pepper.

4. Ladle chili into mugs or crocks and garnish with dollops of sour cream and Monterey Jack cheese. Serve with Southern Jalapeño Cornbread.

Serves 8 to 10

Southern Jalapeño Cornbread

2 cups	sifted all-purpose flour		2 to 3	jalapeño peppers, seeded and finely chopped
1 cup	sugar			
2 tbsp.	baking powder		2 cups	milk
1 tsp.	salt		2	eggs, beaten
1 cup	yellow cornmeal		2 tbsp.	melted butter

1. Preheat oven to 400°F. Grease a shallow 13- × 9-inch baking pan.
2. In a large bowl, sift together the flour, sugar, baking powder and salt. Stir in cornmeal and jalapeño.
3. Stir in milk and beaten egg. Add melted butter and stir until just mixed.
4. Turn into baking pan. Bake until golden brown and a toothpick inserted in the center comes out clean, about 20 minutes. Cut into squares and serve hot with butter.

Serves 8 to 10

Szechwan Hot and Sour Soup

I have to say that one of my favorite soups is hot and sour, a soup that combines the spice of the Orient with the sour of vinegar. This one will make your mouth pucker and sing.

1/4 cup	vegetable oil	1 cup	sliced shiitake mushrooms
1 tsp.	sesame oil	8 cups	chicken stock
2 tbsp.	chopped fresh ginger	1/4 cup	soy sauce
4 cloves	garlic, chopped	1/4 cup	rice wine vinegar
3	jalapeño peppers, finely chopped	1/4 cup	Thai sweet chili sauce
1	onion, thinly sliced	1 cup	thinly sliced Grilled Butterflied Pork Tenderloin with Wasabi Teriyaki Glazing Sauce (page 165)
1	red bell pepper, thinly sliced		
1	yellow bell pepper, thinly sliced	1 cup	cubed firm tofu
1	large carrot, julienned	3	green onions, thinly sliced diagonally
1 cup	bamboo shoots, julienned		Salt and pepper

1. In a large soup pot, heat the vegetable and sesame oils over medium-high heat. Add the ginger, garlic, jalapeño and onion; sauté until onion is tender, about 4 minutes.
2. Add the red pepper, yellow pepper, carrot, bamboo shoots and shiitake mushrooms. Sauté for another 4 minutes. Add the chicken stock. Bring the soup to a rolling boil.
3. Stir in the soy sauce, vinegar and chili sauce. Adjust these seasonings if necessary to give you the proper balance of hot and sour.
4. Before serving, add the pork, tofu and green onions; heat through. Season to taste with salt and pepper.

Serves 8

Magic Mushroom Soup

Mushrooms are truly magical—some are even hallucinogenic, but that's a whole other story. Here's a rich and creamy soup made with a variety of flavorful mushrooms. Finish this soup with a drizzle of truffle oil for added richness.

4 tbsp.	butter	1 cup	sliced oyster mushrooms
4 cloves	garlic, minced	2 tbsp.	chopped fresh thyme
1	large onion, diced	1/4 cup	all-purpose flour
2 stalks	celery, diced	4 cups	chicken stock
2 cups	sliced shiitake mushrooms	1 cup	heavy cream
1 cup	sliced white mushrooms		Salt and pepper
1 cup	sliced brown cremini mushrooms	2 cups	shredded white Cheddar cheese

1. In a large soup pot, melt the butter over medium-high heat. Sauté the garlic, onion and celery until tender, about 4 minutes. Add all the sliced mushrooms and the thyme; sauté until the mushrooms are tender and almost all of the mushroom liquid has evaporated, 8 to 10 minutes.
2. Reduce heat to medium. Stir in the flour. While stirring, slowly add the chicken stock until fully incorporated. Bring soup to a boil, reduce heat and simmer for 30 minutes, stirring occasionally.
3. Add the cream and return to a boil; season to taste with salt and pepper.
4. Ladle soup into warm bowls and garnish each bowl with 1/4 cup of shredded Cheddar.

Serves 8

Sexy Salads

Rice Noodle Salad with Spicy Sesame Soy Vinaigrette

The key to this spicy salad is the chili-seasoned soy sauce. The vinaigrette can double as a marinade for beef, chicken or shrimp. Look for sambal oelek in Asian markets.

1 lb.	rice vermicelli noodles
6 cups	warm water
4	green onions, thinly sliced
1	red onion, sliced
1	carrot, peeled and julienned
1	green bell pepper, thinly sliced
2 cups	bean sprouts
2 cups	snow peas, trimmed and cut into thin strips
1/2 cup	crushed peanuts, for garnish

Spicy Sesame Soy Vinaigrette

2	green onions, finely chopped
2 cloves	garlic, minced
1/2 cup	rice wine vinegar
1/4 cup	mirin (sweet rice wine)
1/4 cup	chili soy sauce
1/4 cup	honey
2 tbsp.	toasted sesame seeds
2 tbsp.	sambal oelek
1 tbsp.	minced fresh ginger
1 tbsp.	sesame oil
1 tsp.	pepper
3/4 cup	vegetable oil
	Salt

1. Place the rice noodles in a bowl and cover with the warm water. Let stand for 30 to 45 minutes, until noodles are softened. Drain and rinse under cold water. Drain again and set aside.
2. Prepare the vinaigrette: In a medium bowl, whisk together the green onions, garlic, rice wine vinegar, mirin, soy sauce, honey, sesame seeds, sambal oelek, ginger, sesame oil and pepper. Slowly whisk in the vegetable oil in a steady stream and whisk until incorporated. Season to taste with salt.
3. In a large bowl, combine the noodles, green onions, red onion, carrot, green pepper, bean sprouts and snow peas. Pour over 1/2 cup of the vinaigrette and toss to mix. Season to taste with pepper. Serve garnished with crushed peanuts.

Serves 6 to 8

Tropical Coleslaw

Good dark rum is what adds the punch to this salad. While on the set of King of the Q, *my co-host thought I was nuts when I added rum to this dressing. But no combination is ridiculous—just different.*

4	green onions, thinly sliced	1/4 cup	white vinegar
2	carrots, shredded	1/4 cup	pineapple juice
1	small green cabbage, thinly sliced	2 tbsp.	Dijon mustard
		2 tbsp.	dark rum
1	ripe mango, peeled and diced	1 tbsp.	sugar
1	red onion, sliced	2 tsp.	toasted cumin seeds
2 cups	diced fresh pineapple	1/2 cup	vegetable oil
2 tbsp.	chopped fresh cilantro	Pinch	cayenne pepper
2	shallots, finely chopped		Salt and pepper

1. In a large bowl, combine the green onions, carrots, cabbage, mango, red onion, pineapple and cilantro.
2. In a small bowl, whisk together the shallots, vinegar, pineapple juice, mustard, rum, sugar and cumin seeds. While whisking, add the oil in a steady stream, whisking until incorporated. Season to taste with cayenne, salt and pepper.
3. Add dressing to cabbage mixture and toss to fully mix. Season to taste with salt and pepper. Cover and refrigerate for 1 hour.

Serves 6 to 8

Barley and Corn Salad

Barley is not just for soup. It is wonderful as a warm side dish to grilled chicken, lamb or beef—and in this salad!

4 cups	water		1/3 cup	vegetable oil
1 tsp.	salt		1/4 cup	white wine vinegar
1 1/2 cups	quick-cooking barley		2 tbsp.	chopped fresh mixed herbs
4 ears	corn, shucked		1 tbsp.	chopped fresh garlic
1	large red onion, thinly sliced		2 tsp.	Bone Dust BBQ Spice (page 99)
4	green onions, thinly sliced			Salt and pepper
1 cup	peas			

1. In a medium saucepan, bring the water and salt to a rolling boil. Add the barley. Cook until tender, 20 to 30 minutes. Drain and cool.
2. Meanwhile, preheat grill to high.
3. Grill the ears of corn and red onion slices until slightly charred and tender, turning frequently. Remove from grill and let cool. Cut the corn kernels from the cob and dice the onion.
4. In a large bowl, combine the barley, corn, red onion, green onions, peas, oil, vinegar, herbs, garlic and Bone Dust BBQ Spice. Mix thoroughly. Season to taste with salt and pepper.
5. Chill before serving.

Serves 8

Cucumber and Radish Salad with Yogurt Dressing

My grandmother used to prepare this salad for me on hot summer days at the cottage. She would go to a local farmer and pick his best produce as well as ask him for his unpasteurized homemade yogurt. It was a delicious salad.

1 bunch	radishes, thinly sliced	1/4 cup	chopped fresh dill
6	green onions, thinly sliced	1 1/2 cups	yogurt
1	red onion, sliced	2 tbsp.	lemon juice
1	large seedless cucumber, peeled and thinly sliced		Salt and freshly ground black pepper

1. In a bowl, combine the radishes, green onions, red onion, cucumber and dill. Stir in the yogurt and lemon juice; season to taste with salt and pepper.
2. Chill before serving.

Serves 6

Turkish Wedding Rice Salad

Turkish Wedding Rice is a hot dish that is thought to bring good luck to newlyweds. It is also thought to be an aphrodisiac. Any food that stimulates the heart and loins is a must! My version is in the form of a salad, cooling for the summer.

1 1/2 cups	long-grain rice		1	red bell pepper, diced
3 cups	water		1/2 cup	toasted pine nuts
1 tsp.	salt		1/2 cup	currants or raisins
3	boneless, skinless chicken breasts (each 6 oz.)		1/4 cup	dried cranberries
			1/4 cup	chopped fresh parsley
2 tbsp.	Bone Dust BBQ Spice (page 99)		1 tbsp.	chopped fresh oregano
			2 tsp.	cinnamon
3	green onions, diced			Salt and pepper
1	onion, diced			

1. In a medium saucepan, bring the rice, water and salt to a boil. Remove from heat, cover and let stand for 1 hour or until the rice is tender. Transfer rice to a cookie sheet and spread out evenly. Let cool completely.
2. Preheat grill to medium-high.
3. Rub chicken breasts with Bone Dust BBQ Spice, pressing the spices into the meat. Grill chicken until fully cooked, about 5 minutes per side. Remove from grill and let cool.
4. Dice the chicken and put it in a large bowl. Add the rice, green onions, onion, red pepper, pine nuts, currants, cranberries, parsley, oregano and cinnamon. Season to taste with salt and pepper.
5. Chill before serving.

Serves 8

Antipasto Olive Salad

This chunky salad is wonderful on its own or as a filling for a great sandwich. If you want a little extra heat, add diced jalapeño or pickled peperoncini.

2	zucchini		2 cups	marinated artichokes, drained and quartered
	Olive oil		2 cups	diced mozzarella cheese
	Salt and pepper to taste		1 cup	gherkin pickles, drained and cut in half lengthwise
1	red onion, diced			
1	red bell pepper, diced		1/4 cup	capers, drained
1	yellow bell pepper, diced		1/4 cup	red wine vinegar
3 cloves	garlic, minced		1/4 cup	olive oil
2 cups	pimento-stuffed green olives, sliced		1 tbsp.	chopped fresh oregano
2 cups	black olives, pitted and sliced			

1. Preheat grill to medium-high.
2. Cut the zucchini lengthwise into 1/2-inch-thick slices. Brush slices with olive oil and season with salt and pepper. Grill zucchini until lightly charred and tender, 4 to 5 minutes per side. Remove from grill and let cool. Cut into 1/2-inch cubes.
3. In a large bowl, combine the zucchini, onion, red pepper, yellow pepper, garlic, green olives, black olives, artichokes, mozzarella, gherkins, capers, vinegar, olive oil and oregano. Season to taste with salt and pepper. Mix thoroughly.

Serves 6 to 8

Multi-Bean Salad with Bacon and Warm Honey Mustard Dressing

Multi-bean salads are delicious. This combination of fresh green and yellow wax beans with firm dried beans is a real treat. If you don't have time to cook dried beans, use canned ones. Rinse them under cold water and drain them well.

1/2 cup	dried red kidney beans	2 tbsp.	chopped fresh parsley
1/2 cup	dried white navy beans	3 cloves	garlic, minced
1/2 cup	dried chick peas	1/2 cup	olive oil
1/2 cup	dried black-eyed peas	1/4 cup	old-fashioned grainy mustard
1 lb.	green beans, trimmed	1/4 cup	honey
1 lb.	yellow wax beans, trimmed	1/4 cup	cider vinegar
1	onion, sliced		Hot sauce
1	red bell pepper, sliced		Salt and pepper
12 slices	bacon, diced and fried crisp		

1. Place the kidney beans, navy beans, chick peas and black-eyed peas in a large saucepan and cover with cold water. Let stand for 24 hours. Drain beans and rinse under cold running water. Return beans to saucepan and cover with cold water. Bring to a boil, reduce heat and simmer, uncovered and stirring occasionally, until tender, 45 minutes to 1 hour. Drain and rinse under cold running water until cool. Drain again.
2. Meanwhile, blanch the green and yellow wax beans in a pot of boiling salted water for 2 minutes. Drain and cool under cold running water. Drain again.
3. In a large bowl, combine the cooked dried beans, blanched beans, onion, red pepper, bacon and parsley.
4. In a small saucepan, combine the garlic, olive oil, mustard, honey and vinegar. Season to taste with hot sauce, salt and pepper. Pour hot dressing over bean salad, toss well and serve immediately.

Serves 8 to 10

Roquefort Grilled Potato Salad with Creamy Smoked Garlic Dressing

Blue cheese and grilled potatoes are a perfect mix. Serve this salad hot off the grill so that the cheese melts and the salad gets sticky. Serve with grilled steaks or tasty burgers.

2 lb.	mini new potatoes	2	green apples, cut into 1/2-inch cubes
	Salt and pepper to taste	1	green bell pepper, diced
1/4 cup	olive oil	1 1/2 cups	crumbled Roquefort cheese
1	large red onion, sliced	1 cup	Creamy Smoked Garlic Dressing (recipe follows)
4	green onions, sliced		
2 stalks	celery, thinly sliced		

1. Cut the potatoes in half and place in a large saucepan. Cover with cold water and bring to a boil over high heat. Add salt. Reduce heat to low and simmer potatoes for 15 minutes or until just tender. Drain and let cool.
2. Preheat grill to medium-high.
3. Toss the potatoes with olive oil, salt and pepper. Place in a grill basket. Grill potatoes for 6 to 8 minutes per side or until lightly grilled and charred. Carefully transfer potatoes to a large bowl. Add red onion, green onions, celery, apples, green pepper, Roquefort and Creamy Smoked Garlic Dressing. Season to taste with salt and pepper. Mix thoroughly and serve immediately.

Serves 6 to 8

Lots of smoked garlic makes this a great dressing for potato and pasta salads. You can never have enough garlic in a dressing.

Creamy Smoked Garlic Dressing

1 head	smoked garlic (8 to 12 cloves) (page 96) or roasted garlic (page 97)	1/4 cup	chopped fresh parsley
1 cup	mayonnaise	1/4 cup	apple cider vinegar
1 cup	sour cream	2 tbsp.	Dijon mustard
1/2 cup	grated Parmesan cheese	1 tbsp.	lemon juice
		1 tbsp.	Worcestershire sauce
			Salt and pepper to taste

1. Peel the garlic cloves and mash until smooth.
2. In a large bowl, whisk together the garlic, mayonnaise, sour cream, Parmesan, parsley, vinegar, mustard, lemon juice, Worcestershire sauce, salt and pepper.
3. Transfer to a sealed container and refrigerate until needed. Will keep up to 1 week.

Makes about 3 cups

Grilled Vegetable Salad with Maple Balsamic Vinaigrette and Goat Cheese

You can grill virtually any kind of vegetable. To grill root vegetables, first blanch in boiling water until tender. For softer vegetables (peppers, eggplant, zucchini), season with oil, vinegar, salt and pepper and grill until lightly charred. Mushrooms are my favorite grilled vegetable, and the grill adds a big boost of flavor to any mushroom.

1	large sweet onion, sliced	**Maple Balsamic Vinaigrette**	
2	zucchini, thinly sliced	1/4 cup	balsamic vinegar
8	large mushrooms, quartered	3 tbsp.	maple syrup
2	red bell peppers, sliced	2 tbsp.	Dijon mustard
1 bunch	asparagus, cut into 2-inch pieces	1 tbsp.	chopped fresh thyme
1 tbsp.	Bone Dust BBQ Spice (page 99)	1/2 cup	olive oil
2 tbsp.	olive oil		Salt and pepper
1/2 cup	crumbled goat cheese		
1 tbsp.	chopped fresh thyme		
	Salt and pepper		

1. In a large bowl, toss all of the vegetables together. Season with Bone Dust BBQ Spice and olive oil. Toss again to coat. Place vegetables in a grill basket.
2. Preheat grill to medium-high.
3. Meanwhile, prepare the dressing: In a small bowl whisk together the balsamic vinegar, maple syrup, mustard and thyme. Whisk in the olive oil in a slow steady stream until the dressing is emulsified. Season to taste with salt and pepper.
4. Grill vegetables until lightly charred and tender, 8 to 10 minutes per side.
5. Transfer vegetables to a large bowl. Toss with vinaigrette, goat cheese and thyme. Season to taste with salt and pepper.

Serves 8

Three-Tomato, Peach and Mozzarella Salad

Christine Chamberlain, chef for President's Choice, calls this dish the ultimate summer salad. It's extremely refreshing and easy to make. Use as many varieties of tomatoes as you can find.

2	large vine-ripened red tomatoes	8 balls	fresh mozzarella cheese, quartered
2	large vine-ripened yellow tomatoes	1/4 cup	fresh basil leaves, thinly sliced
2	large vine-ripened orange tomatoes	1/4 cup	olive oil
3	ripe peaches, peeled and cut into wedges	3 tbsp.	balsamic vinegar
1	sweet onion, thinly sliced		Salt and freshly ground black pepper
3	green onions, thinly sliced		Fresh basil leaves, for garnish

1. Core the tomatoes and slice each tomato into eight wedges. Place tomatoes in a large bowl and add peaches, sweet onion, green onions, mozzarella cheese and sliced basil.
2. Drizzle with olive oil and balsamic vinegar. Season to taste with salt and pepper.
3. Arrange salad on a serving platter and garnish with basil leaves. Serve immediately.

Serves 6 to 8

Lentil and Crab Salad

I first had this salad in Jamaica while filming King of the Q. *It was loaded with fresh crab and green lentils. My version adds some bite with jalapeños and Dijon. Serve with grilled shrimp or salmon.*

2	cans (each 14 oz.) cooked green lentils, drained and rinsed	1	large green jalapeño pepper, seeded and diced
1 cup	fresh lump crab meat	4 cloves	garlic, minced
1	red onion, sliced	1/4 cup	Dijon mustard
1	leek, cut in half lengthwise and cleaned well	1/4 cup	olive oil
1	yellow bell pepper, diced	2 tbsp.	chopped fresh parsley
4	green onions, thinly sliced	2 tbsp.	lemon juice
		2 tbsp.	white wine vinegar
			Salt and pepper

1. In a large bowl, combine the lentils, crab meat, red onion, leek, yellow pepper, green onions, jalapeño and garlic.
2. In a small bowl, whisk together the mustard, oil, parsley, lemon juice and vinegar. Pour over the lentil mixture, season to taste with salt and pepper and mix thoroughly. Cover and refrigerate for 1 hour.

Serves 6 to 8

Steamed Mussel Salad
with Lemon Horseradish

Eaten hot or cold, fresh mussels are tasty little treats. Here, the mussels' sweet and salty flavor takes on the flavors of the marinade. Try this recipe with clams, too.

3 to 5 lb.	fresh mussels	1	red bell pepper, thinly sliced
1/4 cup	olive oil	1/4 cup	freshly grated horseradish
4	shallots, sliced	2 tbsp.	chopped fresh parsley
4 cloves	garlic, minced	2 tbsp.	grainy mustard
1	jalapeño pepper, seeded and diced	2 tbsp.	lemon juice
		1 tbsp.	chopped fresh thyme
1/4 cup	white wine		Salt and pepper to taste
1	onion, sliced		
1	leek, cut in half lengthwise, cleaned well and thinly sliced		

1. Clean and beard the mussels. Set aside.
2. In a large pot, heat the oil over high heat. Add the shallots, garlic and jalapeño; sauté for 2 to 3 minutes or until tender. Stir in the mussels and white wine. Cover and let mussels steam for 5 to 6 minutes or until the shells have opened. Transfer mussels and broth to a large bowl. Discard any mussels that did not open.
3. Add the onion, leek, red pepper, horseradish, parsley, mustard, lemon juice, thyme, salt and pepper. Mix thoroughly. Let cool, then cover and refrigerate for at least 2 hours.
4. To serve, pour mussel salad onto a serving platter and dig in.

Serves 4 to 6

Shrimp and Avocado Pineapple Boats

Large ripe golden pineapples give this salad a burst of sweetness. If you wish, grill slices of pineapple and glaze with a mixture of rum and maple syrup. The char flavors of the grill complement the pineapple beautifully.

2	ripe pineapples		Salt and pepper
1	red onion, diced	1 lb.	large shrimp (20 to 30), peeled and deveined
2 stalks	celery, diced		
2	avocados, peeled and diced	2 tbsp.	Bay Seasoning (page 101)
3	green onions, chopped	2 tsp.	curry powder
1 cup	mayonnaise	1 tsp.	ground cumin
2 tbsp.	lemon juice	1/4 cup	lemon juice
1 tbsp.	chopped fresh dill	1/4 cup	olive oil

1. Cut the pineapples in half from top to bottom. Scoop out the pineapple from each half to make a boat with walls about 1/2 inch thick. Dice the pineapple.
2. In a bowl, combine 2 cups of the diced pineapple, the red onion, celery, avocados, green onions, mayonnaise, lemon juice and dill. Season to taste with salt and pepper. Set aside.
3. Preheat grill to medium-high.
4. In a bowl, toss together the shrimp, Bay Seasoning, curry powder, cumin, lemon juice and olive oil.
5. Grill seasoned shrimp, basting with any remaining olive oil mixture, until just cooked through, 2 to 3 minutes per side. Toss shrimp with pineapple mixture.
6. Spoon salad into the 4 pineapple boats. Serve immediately.

Serves 4 as a main course, 8 sharing a starter

Cabbage, Smoked Ham and Cheddar Salad with Roasted Red Pepper Vinaigrette

Use a really good quality smoked ham for this salad. When I have the time I like to smoke my own hams over corncobs or cracked pecans, which add a sweet nutty flavor to the ham.

1	small Savoy cabbage, thinly sliced	**Roasted Red Pepper Vinaigrette**	
1	red onion, thinly sliced	2	red bell peppers, roasted, peeled and seeded
4	green onions, thinly sliced	2 cloves	garlic, minced
1	red bell pepper, thinly sliced	2 tbsp.	Dijon mustard
12 oz.	smoked ham, cut into strips	1/4 cup	red wine vinegar
2 cups	diced medium Cheddar cheese	1 tbsp.	crushed red chilies
1 tbsp.	chopped fresh sage	3 tbsp.	olive oil
			Salt and pepper

1. In a large bowl, combine the cabbage, red onion, green onions, red pepper, ham, cheese and sage. Set aside.
2. To make the vinaigrette, in a food processor, purée the roasted red peppers and garlic. Add the mustard, vinegar and crushed chilies. With the motor running, slowly add the olive oil in a steady stream until the dressing is emulsified. Season to taste with salt and pepper.
3. Pour dressing over salad. Adjust seasoning. Chill for 1 hour before serving.

Serves 8

Grilled Chicken Salad with Fire-Roasted Tomato Jalapeño Vinaigrette

Tender chicken and ripe avocado is a refreshing blend. If you want to make this salad ahead, don't add the croutons until just before serving.

4	boneless, skinless chicken breasts (each 6 oz.)	**Fire-Roasted Tomato Jalapeño Vinaigrette**		
2 tbsp.	Bone Dust BBQ Spice (page 99)	6	plum tomatoes	
	Vegetable oil	4	jalapeño peppers	
1	sweet onion, cut into 1-inch chunks	1	small onion, cut into wedges	
2	red bell peppers, cut into 1-inch chunks	1/4 cup	olive oil	
		3 tbsp.	red wine vinegar	
1	avocado, peeled and diced	3 tbsp.	water	
4	green onions, sliced	1 tbsp.	chopped fresh oregano	
2 cups	croutons (homemade or store-bought)	2 cloves	garlic, minced	
			Salt and pepper	

1. Preheat grill to medium-high.
2. Season the chicken with Bone Dust BBQ Spice, pressing the spices into the meat. Brush with oil. Grill for 5 to 6 minutes per side or until fully cooked and lightly charred. Remove from grill and let cool.
3. Make the vinaigrette: Grill-roast the tomatoes, jalapeño peppers and onion for 10 to 15 minutes, turning occasionally, until charred and tender. (Be careful when turning the tomatoes, as they will be soft.) Remove from grill and let cool. Peel the tomatoes. Peel and seed the jalapeño peppers.
4. In a food processor, pulse the tomatoes, jalapeño peppers, onion, oil, vinegar, water, oregano and garlic. Season to taste with salt and pepper. Set aside.
5. Cut the chicken into 1-inch chunks and put in a large bowl. Add sweet onion, red peppers, avocado, green onions and croutons. Add dressing and season to taste with salt and pepper. Toss well. Let stand for 15 minutes before serving.

Serves 6 to 8

Luxurious Appetizers

Ultimate BBQ Dip for Chips

Buy chips, make dip, dunk chips and eat. Repeat, repeat, repeat...

1 cup	softened cream cheese	2	green onions, chopped
3/4 cup	sour cream	1 tbsp.	Bone Dust BBQ Spice (page 99)
1/4 to 1/2 cup	hickory smoke–flavored BBQ sauce	1 tsp.	Worcestershire sauce
1 tbsp.	maple syrup		Your favorite chips and crudités
2	shallots, diced		

1. In a food processor, blend the cream cheese, sour cream, BBQ sauce and maple syrup until smooth. Add the shallots, green onions, Bone Dust BBQ Spice and Worcestershire sauce. Pulse until fully mixed. Transfer to a serving bowl and chill.
2. Serve with chips and vegetables.

Makes about 2 1/2 cups

Grilled Eggplant Antipasto Bundles

This is an easy hors d'oeuvre that you can prepare in advance so that you too can enjoy the party.

1	large firm eggplant	1/4 cup	chopped oil-packed sun-dried tomatoes
1/4 cup + 1 tbsp.	balsamic vinegar	2 tbsp.	chopped flat-leaf parsley
1/4 cup	olive oil	1 tbsp.	chopped fresh basil
1 tbsp.	Bone Dust BBQ Spice (page 99)		Salt and pepper to taste
2	green onions, chopped	2 to 3	large vine-ripened tomatoes
1	shallot, finely chopped		Fresh basil leaves and freshly grated Parmesan cheese, for garnish
3/4 cup	goat cheese		

1. Cut 1/2 inch off the top and bottom of the eggplant. Stand the eggplant upright and cut it into eight 1/4-inch-thick slices. Rinse eggplant slices under cold water. Place eggplant slices in a bowl and add 1/4 cup of the balsamic vinegar, the olive oil and Bone Dust BBQ Spice. Toss gently to coat evenly. Let marinate for 15 minutes.
2. Meanwhile, preheat grill to medium-high.
3. Remove eggplant from marinade (reserving any remaining marinade). Grill eggplant slices until cooked through and lightly charred, 4 to 5 minutes per side. Remove from grill, brush with reserved marinade and let cool.
4. Preheat oven to 325°F.
5. In a small bowl, combine the green onions, shallot, goat cheese, sun-dried tomatoes, parsley, basil, remaining 1 tbsp. of balsamic vinegar, salt and pepper. Spread a heaping tablespoon of the goat cheese mixture evenly over each eggplant slice. Roll eggplant up tightly from the thin end. Secure with a toothpick if necessary.
6. Arrange eggplant bundles on a baking sheet. Bake bundles just until the cheese starts to melt, 5 to 10 minutes.
7. To serve, slice each tomato into eight 1/2-inch-thick slices. Arrange tomatoes on plates or a platter. Drizzle tomatoes with olive oil and balsamic vinegar. Top each with a warmed eggplant bundle. Garnish with basil leaves and Parmesan cheese.

Serves 4 to 8

Portobello Mushrooms Stuffed with BBQ Pulled Pork

These stuffed mushrooms can be a perfect appetizer or even a main course.

8	large Portobello mushroom caps	**Stuffing**	
		1	red onion, lightly grilled and sliced
Marinade		4	green onions, sliced
4 cloves	garlic, minced	1	red bell pepper, diced
1½ cups	vegetable oil	1	green bell pepper, diced
1½ cups	apple cider vinegar	4 cups	shredded cheese (Cheddar and Monterey Jack)
1 cup	maple syrup	2 cups	pulled Redneck Riviera Smoked Boston Butt (page 168)
1 cup	gourmet BBQ sauce		
2 tbsp.	Herb Mustard Rub (page 104)	½ cup	gourmet BBQ sauce
		¼ cup	maple syrup
		2 tbsp.	Herb Mustard Rub (page 104)

1. Soak mushroom caps in hot water for 1 hour. Drain on paper towels.
2. Make the marinade: In a large bowl, whisk together the garlic, oil, vinegar, maple syrup, BBQ sauce and herb rub. Add mushroom caps, turning to coat well. Let marinate for 1 hour.
3. Preheat grill to medium-high.
4. Grill mushrooms gill side up, turning once, until lightly charred and tender, 4 to 5 minutes per side. Let cool. Reduce grill temperature to medium.
5. Make the stuffing: In a medium bowl, stir together the red onion, green onions, red pepper, green pepper, cheese, pulled pork, BBQ sauce, maple syrup and herb rub. Using a ½-cup ice cream scoop, top each mushroom cap with a scoop of the stuffing.
6. Return mushrooms to the hot grill. Close the lid and bake until stuffing is hot, 10 to 12 minutes.

Serves 8

Grilled Prosciutto-Wrapped Figs Stuffed with Gorgonzola and Walnuts

Use only fresh figs for this starter. Dried figs will overcook and be tough on the grill.

8	large ripe Black Mission or green figs	1 tbsp.	balsamic vinegar
1/2 cup	crumbled Gorgonzola cheese, softened	2 tsp.	chopped fresh rosemary
			Salt and freshly ground black pepper
1/4 cup	walnut pieces	8 slices	prosciutto
2 tbsp.	honey		

1. Preheat grill to medium-high.
2. Cut the stem off of the figs and cut the figs three-quarters of the way down through the center. Do not cut all the way through.
3. In a small bowl, combine the Gorgonzola, walnuts, honey, balsamic vinegar and rosemary. Season to taste with salt and pepper. Divide the cheese mixture into 8 equal portions. Stuff each fig with the cheese mixture, pressing lightly to fill the fig cavity. Carefully wrap each fig with 1 slice of prosciutto.
4. Place the figs on the grill with the cheese filling facing upwards. Grill for 3 to 4 minutes to crisp the prosciutto. Carefully move the figs to a cool part of the grill. Close the lid and bake the figs until the cheese is melting and the prosciutto is crispy, about 5 minutes.
5. Serve the figs with baby greens and drizzled with balsamic vinegar.

Serves 4 to 8

Grill-Roasted Sweet Pepper and Goat Cheese Bruschetta

This is a favorite around the backyard grill. It's easy to prepare and is a perfect starter to any party. This dish is also great with grilled mushrooms, eggplant or peaches.

1	red bell pepper	2 tbsp.	balsamic vinegar
1	yellow bell pepper	1 tbsp.	chopped fresh oregano
1	orange bell pepper	1 tbsp.	lemon juice
1	green bell pepper		Salt and pepper to taste
1	small red onion, quartered	8	3/4-inch-thick slices rustic Italian bread
3 cloves	garlic, minced		
1/4 cup	olive oil	1 cup	soft creamy goat cheese

1. Preheat grill to medium-high.
2. Grill-roast peppers and onion, turning occasionally, until the peppers are charred black and blistered and the onion is lightly charred and tender, 10 to 15 minutes.
3. Transfer hot peppers to a large bowl and cover with plastic wrap. Let stand for 10 minutes. Peel and seed peppers and pat dry with paper towels. Cut peppers into 1/2-inch-thick slices. Return to bowl. Thinly slice the onion and add to peppers. Add the garlic, oil, vinegar, oregano, lemon juice, salt and pepper. Toss well.
4. Grill bread slices for 1 to 2 minutes per side or until crisp. Spread each slice with a heaping tablespoon of goat cheese. Sprinkle with black pepper. Top with the roasted pepper mixture. Drizzle with extra olive oil and balsamic vinegar.

Serves 8

Cedar-Planked Brie with Oyster Mushroom and Roasted Garlic Crust

I have a similar recipe in my cookbook Sticks and Stones: The Art of Grilling on Plank, Vine and Stone. *For your next party, plank a few wheels of Brie and watch your guests go crazy. This is a showstopper and one of my personal favorites.*

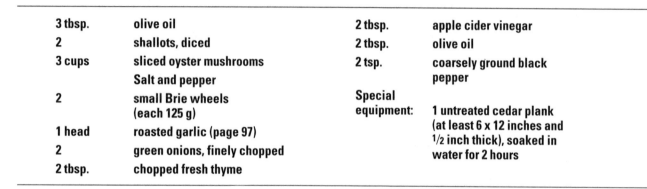

3 tbsp.	olive oil	2 tbsp.	apple cider vinegar
2	shallots, diced	2 tbsp.	olive oil
3 cups	sliced oyster mushrooms	2 tsp.	coarsely ground black pepper
	Salt and pepper		
2	small Brie wheels (each 125 g)	Special equipment:	1 untreated cedar plank (at least 6 x 12 inches and 1/2 inch thick), soaked in water for 2 hours
1 head	roasted garlic (page 97)		
2	green onions, finely chopped		
2 tbsp.	chopped fresh thyme		

1. Heat the oil in a large frying pan over medium-high heat. Cook the shallots and mushrooms, stirring occasionally, until the mushrooms are tender, 5 to 6 minutes. Season with salt and pepper to taste. Let cool.
2. Preheat the grill to high.
3. Cut the top rind off the Brie.
4. In a bowl, mash the roasted garlic with a fork. Stir in the sautéed mushrooms, green onions, thyme, vinegar, oil, pepper and salt to taste. Spread the mushroom mixture evenly over the Brie wheels.
5. Place the plank on the grill and close the lid. Let the plank heat until it starts to crackle, 5 to 7 minutes. (If the wood catches fire, use a spray bottle of water to put out the flames.) Carefully open the lid (it will be smoky) and place the cheese on the plank. Close the lid and bake the cheese until it begins to melt and bubble, 8 to 10 minutes.
6. Remove planked cheese from the grill. Serve with fresh baguettes and plenty of napkins. This is truly oooeey-gooeey good.

Serves 8

Grilled Shrimp with Mango Chutney

Use jumbo shrimp for this recipe. Larger shrimp tend to be a little more forgiving on the grill and will not overcook too quickly.

24	jumbo shrimp (1½ to 2 lb.), peeled and deveined	1 tsp.	cinnamon
		¼ tsp.	nutmeg
			Salt to taste

Mango Chutney

2	ripe mangos, peeled and diced
2	small red chilies, finely chopped
½ cup	sugar
½ cup	water
2 tbsp.	chopped fresh ginger
2 tbsp.	lemon juice
1 tsp.	black pepper

Marinade and Baste

4 cloves	garlic, minced
¼ cup	vegetable oil
¼ cup	Grand Marnier
¼ cup	mango juice or orange juice
1 tbsp.	chopped fresh thyme
1 tbsp.	Bay Seasoning (page 101)
2 tsp.	curry powder
1 tsp.	crushed red chilies

1. To make the chutney, in a medium saucepan over medium-high heat, combine the mangos, chilies, sugar, water, ginger, lemon juice, black pepper, cinnamon, nutmeg and salt. Bring to a boil, reduce heat to medium-low, and simmer, stirring occasionally, until chutney is thick, about 15 minutes. Let cool.
2. To make the marinade, in a small bowl, whisk together the garlic, oil, Grand Marnier, mango juice, thyme, Bay Seasoning, curry powder and crushed chilies. Add shrimp, stirring to coat. Marinate for 20 minutes.
3. Meanwhile, soak 24 bamboo skewers in water for 20 minutes. Preheat grill to medium-high.
4. Skewer 1 shrimp onto the end of each bamboo skewer. Reserve marinade for basting. Grill shrimp, basting with reserved marinade, until opaque and just firm to the touch, 3 to 4 minutes per side. Serve immediately with mango chutney for dipping.

Serves 8

Jamaica Roadside Shrimp Boil

While traveling around Jamaica I grabbed every opportunity to devour tasty bags of peppery roadside shrimp. Even though these shrimp aren't fresh out of the fishing nets, here's my delicious version. Buy live shrimp if you can find them. They have the most flavor, and it's a lot of fun to eat them whole. Pull the head from the body and suck the head for all its salty goodness, then peel the body and eat the meat.

1	onion, sliced	4 cups	water
1	Scotch bonnet pepper, sliced	1/4 cup	Bone Dust BBQ Spice (page 99)
4 cloves	garlic, chopped	2 tbsp.	salt
2 sprigs	fresh thyme	2 lb.	jumbo shrimp, unpeeled
2 bottles	beer		

1. In a large soup pot over high heat, bring the onion, Scotch bonnet pepper, garlic, thyme, beer, water, Bone Dust BBQ Spice and salt to a rolling boil.
2. Add the shrimp and boil until the shrimp are just cooked through and firm to the touch, 8 to 10 minutes.
3. Drain the shrimp and serve immediately with lemon wedges and plenty of napkins.

Serves 4 to 6

Smoked Scallops with Prosciutto, Pistachios and Three-Citrus Salsa

Scallops smoked in a conventional smoker have a firm but tender texture and golden brown color. If you do not have a smoker, grill the scallops until just cooked through, 2 to 3 minutes per side. Let cool and then follow the remaining instructions.

Buy large, firm scallops and ask for the freshest available. Make sure they have not been packed in heavy brine.

24	jumbo sea scallops (about 2 lb.)	1	seedless orange
3 tbsp.	Bay Seasoning (page 101)	1/2	small red onion, diced
	Hickory or peach smoking chips	1	jalapeño pepper, seeded and finely diced
16	thin slices prosciutto, torn in half lengthwise	1	red bell pepper, diced
1/2 cup	coarsely crushed pistachios	1	green onion, finely chopped
	Arugula	1 tbsp.	chopped fresh mint
		1 tbsp.	honey
Three-Citrus Salsa		1 tbsp.	lemon juice
1	lemon	1 tbsp.	olive oil
2	limes	1 tsp.	chopped fresh ginger
			Salt and pepper to taste

1. Prepare your smoker according to manufacturer's instructions to a temperature of 175°F.
2. Rub the scallops with the Bay Seasoning, pressing the seasoning into the meat. Arrange scallops on the top rack of the smoker. Close lid and smoke scallops for 1 1/2 to 2 hours, replenishing smoking chips, coals and water as required. Scallops are done when they are firm to the touch and a uniform pearly white color inside. Remove scallops from smoker and let cool.
3. To make the salsa, cut the top and bottom off the lemon, limes and orange. Stand each fruit on one end and cut away the peel and pith from top to bottom. Working over a bowl to catch the juices, cut alongside each membrane to remove the fruit

segments. Squeeze any liquid from the membranes over the fruit. Add the red onion, jalapeños, red pepper, green onion, mint, honey, lemon juice, oil, ginger, salt and pepper. Stir well.

4. To serve, slice each scallop into three rounds. Fan 3 scallops in the center of each plate to form a circle. Fill the center of the scallop ring with 2 tbsp. of salsa. Top with a few ribbons of prosciutto and garnish with crushed pistachios. Arrange some arugula alongside and drizzle the arugula with olive oil.

Serves 8

Champagne Oyster Shooters with Mango Salsa

During a taping of one my King of the Q *episodes, one of my guests proposed to his girlfriend. He dropped to one knee and popped the big question: Do you like oysters? Because if you don't we can't get married. She said yes, and I prepared them their engagement shooters on the beaches of Jamaica.*

Okay, it didn't happen exactly like that, but it was on camera, she said yes, and they had oysters before the question popping.

8	large fresh oysters, ice cold	1 cup	diced peeled mango
	Chilled champagne	1 tbsp.	chopped fresh cilantro
		1 tbsp.	olive oil
Mango Salsa		1 tbsp.	lime juice
1	shallot, finely chopped	1 tsp.	habanero hot sauce
1	green onion, finely chopped		Salt and pepper to taste

1. Prepare the mango salsa by combining the shallot, green onion, mango, cilantro, oil, lime juice, hot sauce, salt and pepper.
2. Shuck the oysters and place 1 oyster in each of 8 shot glasses. Top each oyster with 1 tbsp. of mango salsa.
3. Fill each glass to the brim with champagne. Shoot 'em back. Ask for more and keep on loving.

Serves 2 to 4

Smoked Chicken Wings

Doing your own smoking is quite rewarding and not as difficult as you may think. It does take a little extra patience, but the results are delicious. For this recipe I like to use whole chicken wings, tips attached. Serve these babies with lots of ice-cold beer.

You can find Sriacha chili sauce in Asian food stores.

5 lb.	jumbo whole chicken wings	1/2 cup	gourmet BBQ sauce
1 cup	Bone Dust BBQ Spice (page 99)	1/4 cup	Sriacha chili sauce
	Hickory smoking chips	1/4 cup	melted butter
		2 tbsp.	lemon juice

1. Season the chicken wings with the Bone BBQ Dust Spice, rubbing the spices into the meat. Set aside.
2. Prepare your smoker according to manufacturer's instructions, with about 12 coals. Bring smoker to 200°F. Adjust vents to maintain this temperature.
3. Place chicken wings on the smoker racks, place lid on smoker and add soaked hickory smoking chips. Smoke wings until fully cooked and firm to the touch, 2 1/2 to 3 hours, adding coals, wood chips and water as necessary.
4. While the wings are smoking, prepare the sauce. In a small saucepan over medium heat, whisk together the BBQ sauce, chili sauce, butter and lemon juice. Bring to a low boil and simmer for 5 minutes. Set aside. Just before wings are done, reheat sauce.
5. Remove wings from the smoker and toss in hot BBQ sauce. Consume immediately.

Serves 6 to 8

Sticky Honey Garlic Ginger Chicken Wings

What goes with chicken wings best? Ice-cold frosty beer. With these sticky wings I recommend honey brown lager for the guzzling. Also have lots of wet naps and napkins on hand.

3 lb.	jumbo chicken wings (about 36)	2 tbsp.	finely chopped fresh garlic
		2 tbsp.	lemon juice
1/4 cup	Indonesian Cinnamon Rub (page 105)	2 tsp.	sesame oil
			Salt and pepper to taste
2 tbsp.	vegetable oil	2	green onions, chopped
1/2 cup	honey	1 tbsp.	toasted sesame seeds
1/4 cup	soy sauce		
2 tbsp.	finely chopped fresh ginger		

1. Trim wing tips from chicken wings and save for another use. Cut the wing in half at the joint. Place wing pieces in a large bowl and toss with Indonesian Cinnamon Rub and vegetable oil. Marinate, covered and refrigerated, for 24 hours.
2. To make the sauce, in a large bowl, combine the honey, soy sauce, ginger, garlic, lemon juice, sesame oil, salt and pepper. Set aside.
3. Preheat grill to medium.
4. Place chicken wings in a grill basket. Grill wings, turning every 5 or 6 minutes, until fully cooked, golden brown and crisp, 10 to 12 minutes per side.
5. Remove wings from grill basket and add to the sauce. Add green onions and sesame seeds. Toss well and serve immediately.

Serves 4

Kama Sutra Cinnamon-Skewered Chicken Thighs

This is one of my favorite grilling recipes. The combination of cinnamon and chicken makes for an exotic appetizer worthy of any Kama Sutra lover.

I find my cinnamon sticks for skewering at bulk spice shops and in the bulk section of grocery stores. Prepackaged or jarred cinnamon sticks are usually not long enough.

6	boneless, skin-on chicken thighs	6 cloves	garlic, chopped
2 tbsp.	Indonesian Cinnamon Rub (page 105)	1/2 cup	honey
		1/4 cup	melted butter
12	thin cinnamon sticks, at least 6 inches long	2 tbsp.	curry paste
		1 tbsp.	finely chopped fresh ginger

1. Preheat grill to medium-high.
2. Rub the chicken thighs with the Indonesian Cinnamon Rub, pressing the spices into the meat. Cut the chicken thighs in half lengthwise. Skewer each half onto the end of a cinnamon stick.
3. In a small bowl, whisk together the garlic, honey, butter, curry paste and ginger.
4. Grill the chicken thighs, basting generously with the sauce, until the chicken is fully cooked, 4 to 6 minutes per side.

Serves 6

Grilled BBQ Chicken Quesadillas

Lots of cheese and lots of chicken produces lots of ooey-gooey goodness. Be careful not to burn the tortillas on the grill.

3	boneless, skinless chicken breasts (each 6 oz.)	1	yellow bell pepper, diced
2 tbsp.	Bone Dust BBQ Spice (page 99)	1 tbsp.	chopped fresh cilantro
			Salt and pepper
1 cup	hickory smoke–flavored BBQ sauce	2 cups	shredded Monterey Jack cheese
2 ears	boiled corn on the cob	1 cup	shredded Cheddar cheese
3 cloves	garlic, minced	8	7-inch flour tortillas
1	small red onion, diced		Oil
1	jalapeño pepper, seeded and finely diced		

1. Preheat grill to medium-high.
2. Rub the chicken breasts with Bone Dust BBQ Spice, pressing the spices into the meat. Grill chicken, basting with 1/2 cup of the BBQ sauce, until fully cooked, 5 to 6 minutes per side. Let cool. Thinly slice across the grain. Set aside.
3. Working over a large bowl, slice the corn kernels from the cobs. Add garlic, onion, jalapeño, yellow pepper, cilantro, salt, pepper and 1/4 cup of the BBQ sauce.
4. Brush 4 tortillas with remaining 1/4 cup of BBQ sauce, leaving a 1/2-inch border around the edge. Mix cheeses together. Sprinkle half the cheese over each tortilla. Spread 2 tbsp. of the corn mixture evenly over the cheese. Top with chicken, then remaining corn salsa and cheese. Moisten edges of tortillas with water and top with the remaining tortillas, pressing down firmly on the edges to seal.
5. Preheat grill to medium.
6. Brush each tortilla with oil. Grill tortillas, turning once, until lightly charred and crisp and the cheese is melted, 2 to 4 minutes per side.
7. Let cool for 5 minutes. Cut into wedges and serve with Ultimate BBQ Dip (page 36).

Serves 8

Lamb Chops with Dijon Goat Cheese Dunk

Use small, tender Ontario or New Zealand lamb. The racks tend to have smaller loins, which makes these chops a perfect size for bite-size hors d'oeuvres. This Dijon Goat Cheese Dunk is also good for dunking your favorite body parts.

2	frenched lamb racks (5 to 7 ribs each)	1/4 cup	softened cream cheese
1/4 cup	Great Canadian Steak Spice (page 98)	1/4 cup	maple syrup
		1/4 cup	Dijon mustard
1/4 cup	olive oil	2 tbsp.	lemon juice
1/4 cup	balsamic vinegar	1 tbsp.	chopped fresh rosemary
2 cloves	garlic, minced	1 tbsp.	prepared horseradish
1/2 cup	softened goat cheese		Salt and pepper to taste

1. Cut between rib bones to make chops about 3/4 inch thick. Rub the chops with Great Canadian Steak Spice, pressing the spices into the meat. Place chops in a glass dish large enough to hold them in one layer, and drizzle with olive oil and balsamic vinegar. Turn to coat. Let marinate for 30 minutes.
2. Meanwhile, in a small bowl, stir together the garlic, goat cheese, cream cheese, maple syrup, mustard, lemon juice, rosemary, horseradish, salt and pepper. Transfer to a serving bowl.
3. Preheat grill to medium-high.
4. Grill lamb chops for 3 to 5 minutes per side for medium doneness. Transfer to a serving platter.
5. To enjoy, dunk the chops into the Dijon Goat Cheese Dunk.

Serves 4 to 6

Peach and Pork Satays

When grilling satays, place the meat over the heat near the edge of the grill, leaving the exposed bamboo skewer hanging off the edge of the grill. This will allow you to turn the skewers easily without burning your fingertips.

2 lb.	pork tenderloin, trimmed			Cracked black pepper
4 cloves	garlic, minced		8 slices	bacon, partially cooked
1/2 cup	Southern Comfort		1 cup	gourmet BBQ sauce
1/2 cup	peach or orange juice			
2 tbsp.	Bone Dust BBQ Spice (page 99)		**Southern Dipping Sauce**	
2 tbsp.	vegetable oil		1/4 cup	Southern Comfort
1 tbsp.	chopped fresh oregano		1 cup	gourmet BBQ sauce
1 tbsp.	crushed red chilies		Dash or two	hot sauce
2	ripe peaches, each cut into 8 wedges			

1. Soak 16 bamboo skewers in water for 30 minutes. (Or use metal skewers.)
2. Slice each tenderloin crosswise into eight 1- to 2-inch chunks (each about 2 oz.). Press firmly on each slice to slightly flatten.
3. In a glass dish large enough to hold the pork in one layer, whisk together the garlic, Southern Comfort, peach juice, Bone Dust BBQ Spice, oil, oregano, and chilies. Add pork, turning to coat. Marinate, covered and refrigerated, for 2 hours.
4. Preheat grill to medium-high.
5. Season the peach wedges with cracked black pepper. Cut each piece of bacon in half and wrap one half around each peach wedge. Skewer 1 peach piece onto each skewer.
6. Remove pork from marinade (reserving marinade) and skewer 1 piece of pork onto each skewer, keeping it tight against the peach.
7. To make the dipping sauce, in a small bowl, whisk together the Southern Comfort BBQ sauce and hot sauce.
8. Grill satays, basting with the sauce, until the pork is just cooked through and the bacon is crisp, 3 to 4 minutes per side. Serve with dipping sauce.

Makes 16 satays

Grill-Roasted Kielbasa with Apricot Mustard Glaze

My friend Duane in Chicago introduced me to this treat. I was a little skeptical at first, but it turns out to be a perfect party pleaser.

1-lb. piece	Polish kielbasa (8 to 12 inches)	¼ cup	honey
		¼ cup	prepared mustard
		2 tbsp.	water
Apricot Mustard Glaze		1 tbsp.	chopped fresh parsley
½ cup	apricot jam		Salt and pepper

1. To make the glaze, in a medium saucepan over medium-high heat, whisk together the apricot jam, honey, mustard, water and parsley until smooth. Remove from heat. Season to taste with salt and pepper.
2. Preheat grill to medium-high.
3. Grill the kielbasa until lightly charred and just starting to crisp, 3 to 4 minutes per side. Transfer to a cutting board.
4. Slice the kielbasa every ¼ inch about ¾ of the way through. This is to allow the center of the kielbasa to get hot. Place the kielbasa on the upper level of the grill or to the side for indirect cooking.
5. Baste kielbasa with the apricot glaze, making sure the glaze gets in between the slices. Close lid and cook, basting occasionally, until the kielbasa is heated through, crispy and heavily glazed, 10 to 15 minutes.
6. Slice into rounds and serve.

Serves 4 to 6

Scrumptious Sides

Grilled Asparagus with Raspberries and Asiago

Tender, sweet asparagus is perfect for the grill. Place the spears across the grill bars to keep them from falling through the grates.

2 bunches	asparagus, trimmed	1 tbsp.	chopped fresh thyme
2 tbsp.	olive oil	1/2 pint	fresh raspberries
2 tbsp.	raspberry-flavored vinegar	1/4 cup	shredded Asiago cheese
	Salt and pepper to taste		

1. Preheat grill to high.
2. In a large bowl, gently toss the asparagus with the oil, vinegar, salt and pepper.
3. Place asparagus across the grill and cook, turning carefully, until tender and crisp, 3 to 5 minutes.
4. Return asparagus to the bowl. Add the thyme; drizzle with extra raspberry vinegar and olive oil. Season to taste with salt and pepper. Toss well.
5. Arrange asparagus on a platter and garnish with fresh raspberries and Asiago cheese.

Serves 8

Down-Home Collard Greens

My first experience with collard greens came while on a culinary expedition to New Orleans. Famed Chef Leah Chase, owner and operator of Dooky Chase Restaurant, prepared this dish for me along with some of the best fried chicken I've ever had. This is my version of her collard greens.

Be sure to wash the greens well to remove grit and sand.

1 bunch	collard greens (1 to 1½ lb.)	¼ cup	chicken stock
2 tbsp.	kosher salt	2 tbsp.	corn syrup
2 tbsp.	vegetable oil	2 tbsp.	cider vinegar
1	onion, diced	2 tbsp.	butter
6 cloves	garlic, minced		Salt and pepper
2	jalapeño peppers, seeded and diced		

1. Cut the stems off the collard greens and discard. Stack the leaves on top of each other. Roll the leaves from the side to form a cigar shape. Thinly slice the collard cigar into a chiffonade.
2. Wash the sliced collards in cold water; drain well. Transfer leaves to a bowl and toss well with kosher salt. Let stand for 15 minutes. Rinse under cold water and drain well. (Use a salad spinner to remove as much moisture as possible.)
3. In a large, deep skillet over medium-high heat, heat the vegetable oil. Sauté the onion, garlic and jalapeño until tender, 3 to 5 minutes. Add collard greens and chicken stock. Bring to a boil, reduce heat and simmer greens for 10 minutes, boiling off excess moisture. Stir in the corn syrup, vinegar and butter. Season to taste with salt and pepper.
4. Serve immediately with your favorite ribs and chicken.

Serves 4 to 6

Marinated Corn on the Cob

One of my clients asked me to develop some new menu items for Lee Roy Selmon's, a restaurant in Tampa, Florida. In one of our "ideation" sessions we got to discussing corn on the cob, and it was said that a restaurant in Nashville served a marinated corn on the cob. Well, into the kitchen we went, and out came this recipe. It is a perfect dish for any picnic or party.

12 ears	peaches and cream corn, unhusked	1 cup	gourmet BBQ sauce
		1 cup	water
¼ cup	olive oil	½ cup	olive oil
1 cup	Bay Seasoning (page 101)	½ cup	apple cider vinegar
		3 tbsp.	Bay Seasoning (page 101)
Marinade		2 tbsp.	lemon juice
1	small onion, diced		
2 cloves	garlic, minced		

1. Pull the husk away from the ear without removing it, and remove the silk. Twist the husk at the base—don't remove it; it makes a handy handle. Rub corn with olive oil and Bay Seasoning. Place on a steamer rack over boiling water and steam corn until just done, about 8 minutes.
2. Make the marinade: In a glass dish large enough to hold the corn, whisk together the onion, garlic, BBQ sauce, water, oil, vinegar, Bay Seasoning and lemon juice.
3. Lay the corn in the marinade, turning to coat, with the husks over the edge of the dish. The marinade should completely cover the corn. Marinate at room temperature for 2 to 4 hours.
4. Serve at room temperature.

Serves 6 to 12

Grilled Portobello Mushroom Fries

Thick wedges of giant Portobello mushrooms make an incredible fry. Or top your burger with them.

8	very large Portobello mushroom caps (5 to 6 inches across)	1/2 cup	balsamic vinegar
		1/4 cup	honey
8 cloves	garlic, minced	2 tbsp.	Bone Dust BBQ Spice (page 99)
1 cup	hickory smoke–flavored BBQ sauce	2 tbsp.	chopped fresh rosemary
1/2 cup	vegetable oil		Coarse salt and cracked black pepper to taste

1. In a large bowl, soak mushrooms in hot water to cover for 1 hour. Drain on paper towels.
2. In the bowl, whisk together the garlic, BBQ sauce, oil, vinegar, honey, Bone Dust BBQ Spice, rosemary, salt and pepper. Slice each mushroom into 1 1/2-inch-wide sticks. Add to marinade and stir to coat well. Let marinate for 15 minutes.
3. Preheat grill to medium-high.
4. Grill mushrooms until tender and lightly charred, 2 to 3 minutes per side. Season with coarse salt and serve immediately.

Serves 4 to 6

Foil-Baked Stuffed Red Onions

I love onions, baked, fried, raw, sautéed, in soup—you name the onion dish and I will eat it. I had my most memorable onion while passing through Vidalia, Georgia, one May. I stopped at a roadside stand and bought a few (hundred) sweet Vidalia onions. I peeled one, sliced it and seasoned it with salt. That was it. Tangy, sweet and delicious.

4	medium-large red onions, peeled	1/4 cup	chopped walnuts
8 slices	bacon, diced and cooked almost crisp	2 tbsp.	cider vinegar
		1 tbsp.	chopped fresh parsley
4 cloves	garlic, minced	Pinch	cayenne pepper
2	green onions, finely chopped		Salt and pepper to taste
1/2 cup	shredded Oka cheese		Olive oil

1. Preheat grill to high.
2. Cut a 1/2-inch-thick slice from the top of each onion and, using a melon-ball cutter, scoop out the center, leaving a shell of about 3 or 4 onion layers.
3. In a bowl, combine bacon, garlic, green onions, Oka, walnuts, vinegar, parsley, cayenne, salt and pepper.
4. Cut 4 sheets of foil about 12 inches square. Brush 1 side of each sheet with oil. Place an onion shell on each sheet. Stuff each of the onions with the cheese mixture, carefully pressing the stuffing firmly into place.
5. Wrap each onion tightly in the foil. Grill, turning occasionally, until the onions are tender, 40 to 50 minutes. Remove from grill and carefully unwrap onions.
6. Cut each onion in half. Serve with T-bone or porterhouse steaks.

Serves 4 to 8

Drunken Peppers

If you like hot peppers on your pizza or as a side to your favorite sandwich, this recipe should make your day hot and spicy.

2 lb.	banana peppers		1 tbsp.	black peppercorns
1 lb.	jalapeño peppers		4 cups	white vinegar
1 lb.	red finger chili peppers		2 cups	water
1	large red onion		1 cup	vodka
2 tbsp.	mustard seeds		1/2 cup	sugar
1 tbsp.	dill seeds		1/2 cup	kosher salt

1. Wash a 4-quart crock or other sealable non-plastic container. Dry thoroughly.
2. Cut the hot peppers and onion into 1/2-inch-thick slices. Place peppers, onion, mustard seeds, dill seeds and peppercorns in the crock.
3. In a large saucepan, bring the vinegar, water, vodka, sugar and salt to a rolling boil. Remove from heat and let cool for 5 minutes.
4. Pour over pepper mixture and stir thoroughly.
5. Let cool completely. Cover and refrigerate for at least 5 days to allow the peppers to pickle.
6. Serve with your favorite sandwiches and burgers. Peppers will keep, refrigerated, for 8 weeks.

Makes a small keg of hot peppers

Spicy Garlic Dill Pickles

When I worked at Rhodes restaurant in Toronto back in the mid-80s, we used to prepare our own crunchy, slightly spicy dill pickles. This is my version of these tasty pickles.

5 lb.	pickling cucumbers (about 5 inches long)	2/3 cup	kosher salt
3	banana peppers	2/3 cup	sugar
4	jalapeño peppers	3 tbsp.	mustard seeds
1	large Spanish onion	2 tbsp.	black peppercorns
16 cloves	garlic, minced	1 tbsp.	coriander seeds
1/2 cup	chopped fresh dill	1 tbsp.	dill seeds
5 cups	white vinegar	1 tbsp.	crushed red chilies
2 1/2 cups	water	3	bay leaves

1. Wash a 5-quart crock or other sealable non-plastic container. Dry thoroughly.
2. Cut the cucumbers lengthwise into 4 or 6 wedges, depending on thickness. Slice the banana and jalapeño peppers into thin rings, seeds and all. Cut the onion into 1/2-inch-thick slices. Place the cucumbers, peppers, onion, garlic and dill in the crock.
3. In a large saucepan, bring the vinegar, water, salt, sugar, mustard seeds, peppercorns, coriander seeds, dill seeds, chilies and bay leaves to a rolling boil. Remove from heat and let cool for 5 minutes.
4. Pour over cucumber mixture and stir thoroughly.
5. Let cool completely. Cover and refrigerate for at least 5 days to allow the cucumbers to pickle.
6. Serve with your favorite sandwiches and burgers. Pickles will keep, refrigerated, for 8 weeks.

Makes a small barrel of pickles

Over-Stuffed Twice-Baked Potatoes

Twice-baked potatoes, loaded with three cheeses, bacon or ham, and green onions, are a creamy and delicious accompaniment to any steak. Try different cheeses, as well as grilled chicken or BBQ pulled pork in place of the ham.

4	large baking potatoes (each 10 to 12 oz.), scrubbed	1/2 cup	crumbled creamy goat cheese
8 cloves	roasted garlic (page 97), mashed	1/2 cup	shredded smoked Gruyère cheese
1	roasted red pepper, peeled, seeded and diced	1/2 cup	shredded mozzarella cheese
3	green onions, chopped	2 tbsp.	butter
1 cup	diced smoked ham	2 tsp.	Bone Dust BBQ Spice (page 99)
			Salt and pepper to taste

1. Preheat oven to 400°F.
2. Bake potatoes on the oven rack until tender, about 1 1/2 hours. Let cool slightly. Do not turn off oven.
3. Cut potatoes in half lengthwise. Carefully scoop out flesh and place in a large bowl, reserving skins on a baking sheet. Mash flesh and add roasted garlic, red pepper, green onions, ham, goat cheese, Gruyère, mozzarella, butter, Bone Dust BBQ Spice, salt and pepper. Mix thoroughly.
4. Spoon potato mixture into the potato skins, pressing firmly to stuff them really well.
5. Return potatoes to oven and bake until heated through, 10 to 15 minutes. Serve immediately.

Serves 8

Goat Cheese Mashed Potatoes with Pulled Pork Gravy

Potatoes can't get any better than this. Rich and creamy mashed potatoes flavored with goat cheese and topped with a BBQ pulled pork gravy. A meal in a bowl.

2 lb.	Yukon Gold potatoes, peeled		1	small red onion, sliced
3 tbsp.	butter		4 cloves	garlic, minced
1/2 cup	heavy cream		2 cups	oyster mushrooms, sliced
1/4 cup	soft creamy goat cheese		2 cups	pulled Redneck Riviera Smoked Boston Butt (page 168)
1/4 cup	finely chopped fresh thyme			
	Salt and pepper to taste		1/2 cup	beef stock
			1 cup	gourmet BBQ sauce
Pulled Pork Gravy			2 tbsp.	malt vinegar
2 tbsp.	butter		Pinch	cayenne pepper

1. In a large pot of boiling salted water, cook the potatoes until tender, 15 to 20 minutes. Drain well and return pot to low heat for 1 minute to dry the potatoes.
2. While the potatoes are cooking, prepare the gravy. Melt 2 tbsp. butter in a large frying pan over medium-high heat. Cook the onion, garlic and mushrooms, stirring occasionally, until the onions are golden brown and the mushrooms tender, 8 to 10 minutes. Season to taste with salt and pepper.
3. Stir in the pulled pork and heat, stirring, for 5 minutes. Whisk together the beef stock and BBQ sauce; stir into the pork mixture. Stir in vinegar, cayenne and salt and pepper to taste. Remove from heat.
4. Mash the potatoes. Beat in 3 tbsp. butter, the cream, goat cheese, thyme, salt and pepper.
5. Spoon mashed potatoes onto 6 plates. With the spoon, make a crater in the center of the potatoes. Fill with gravy and serve immediately.

Serves 6

Mashed Sweet Potatoes with Marshmallow Butter

Marshmallows and butter. Heaven can wait—pass the sweet potatoes.

2 lb.	sweet potatoes	**Marshmallow Butter**	
1/2 cup	heavy cream		
1/4 cup	finely chopped fresh sage	1 cup	mini white marshmallows
1/4 cup	maple syrup	1/2 cup	chopped toasted pecans
3 tbsp.	butter	1/4 cup	butter
	Salt and pepper	2 tbsp.	orange juice
		Pinch	cayenne pepper

1. Peel the sweet potatoes and cut into 3-inch chunks. In a large pot of boiling salted water, boil the sweet potatoes until tender, 15 to 20 minutes. Drain well and return pot to low heat for 1 minute to dry the potatoes.
2. While the sweet potatoes are boiling, prepare the marshmallow butter. In a microwave-safe dish, combine the marshmallows, pecans, butter, orange juice and cayenne pepper. Microwave on High for 1 to 2 minutes until the marshmallows have softened and the butter is melted. Stir mixture together.
3. Mash the sweet potatoes. Beat in the cream, sage, maple syrup and butter. Season to taste with salt and pepper.
4. Spoon the mashed sweet potatoes onto serving plates. With the spoon, make a crater in the center of the potatoes. Spoon 2 tbsp. of marshmallow butter into each crater and serve immediately.

Serves 6 to 8

Stuffed Tomatoes

Big vine-ripened tomatoes are perfect for stuffing. My Pamela grew some tomato monsters one summer. One even weighed in at 2 lb. 2 oz.!

4	ripe field tomatoes	1 tbsp.	finely chopped garlic
1/2 cup	chopped fresh herbs (basil, oregano, parsley)	1 tbsp.	olive oil
1/2 cup	grated Parmesan cheese		Salt and pepper to taste

1. Preheat grill to medium.
2. Cut the tomatoes in half crosswise. Carefully remove and discard the seeds.
3. In a bowl, combine the herbs, Parmesan, garlic, oil, salt and pepper. Fill the tomatoes with the cheese mixture.
4. Grill the tomatoes until tender and the cheese is starting to melt, 8 to 10 minutes.

Makes 8 stuffed tomatoes

Cherry's Spot Rice and Peas

On the highway from Ocho Rios to Kingston in Jamaica there is a row of about 35 roadside food stands that serve everything from jerk chicken, steamed fish and festival (a funky fried dough) to curried goat and jerk pork. My friend Barrington was quite fond of Cherry's Spot and suggested we film a segment there. Well Cherry's makes one hell of a great rice and peas, and this is my take on the recipe.

1/4 cup	vegetable oil	1	bay leaf
1	onion, diced	2 cups	long-grain rice
4 cloves	garlic, minced	1 tbsp.	chopped fresh thyme
1 tbsp.	finely chopped fresh ginger	4 to 5 cups	chicken stock or water
1	green Scotch bonnet pepper, thinly sliced	1/2 cup	coconut milk
		2 cups	cooked kidney beans
4	green onions, chopped		Salt and pepper

1. In a large saucepan, heat the oil over medium heat. Sauté the onion, garlic and ginger until the onion is tender, 3 to 4 minutes. Add the Scotch bonnet pepper, green onions, bay leaf, rice and thyme; cook, stirring, for 2 minutes. Stir in chicken stock and coconut milk. Cover and bring to a boil. Stir in the beans, cover and reduce heat to low. Simmer for 15 to 20 minutes, stirring gently once, until rice is cooked. Season to taste with salt and pepper.
2. Discard bay leaf and serve immediately.

Serves 8 to 10

Bacon and Cheddar Flapjacks

These delicious pancakes can be served at breakfast drizzled with maple syrup or as an appetizer garnished with BBQ pulled pork.

1 cup	all-purpose flour		1 clove	garlic, minced
1/4 cup	corn flour		4 slices	bacon, cooked and chopped
1 tsp.	baking soda		1 cup	shredded Cheddar cheese
1/2 tsp.	salt		1 tsp.	Bone Dust BBQ Spice (page 99)
1	large egg			Pepper to taste
1 cup	whole milk		4 tbsp.	butter
2	green onions, minced			

1. In a bowl, mix together the all-purpose flour, corn flour, baking soda and salt. In a small bowl, whisk together the egg and milk. Slowly whisk the milk mixture into the dry mixture until fully incorporated and there are no lumps. Let rest at room temperature for 2 hours.
2. Fold into the batter the green onions, garlic, bacon, cheese, Bone Dust BBQ Spice and pepper.
3. Melt 1 tbsp. of the butter in a large nonstick frying pan over medium-high heat. Pour 1/4 cup of the batter into the pan for each pancake, making 3 pancakes at a time. Cook until the surface bubbles. Turn the pancakes and cook for 1 to 2 minutes or until golden brown. Repeat until all the batter is used up.

Makes 12 pancakes

The Cheesiest Baked Macaroni and Cheese

If you are watching what you eat, then stay away from this recipe. It's a killer!

1 lb.	macaroni	2 cups	shredded yellow Cheddar cheese
3 tbsp.	butter		
1	small onion, diced	1 tsp.	paprika
1/4 cup	all-purpose flour	1 tsp.	dry mustard
2 1/2 cups	milk	1/2 tsp.	black pepper
1 cup	heavy cream		Salt to taste
1 cup	Velveeta cheese	1 cup	frozen peas
1 cup	shredded white Cheddar cheese	2 cups	crumbled potato chips

1. Preheat oven to 350°F. Grease a 2- to 3-quart casserole dish.
2. In a large pot of boiling salted water, cook the macaroni until it is barely tender. Drain and let cool.
3. In a large saucepan over medium-low heat, melt the butter. Sauté the onion until transparent and tender, 2 to 3 minutes. Stir in the flour until incorporated. Slowly pour in the milk and cream, stirring constantly until the mixture is smooth. Cook, stirring frequently, until sauce is thickened, 10 to 15 minutes.
4. Whisk in the Velveeta and Cheddar cheeses until smooth. Remove from heat and stir in paprika, mustard, pepper and salt.
5. Combine the cooked pasta and the peas in the casserole dish; stir. Pour in the warm cheese sauce and mix thoroughly.
6. Bake until bubbling, 20 to 30 minutes. Sprinkle with the crumbled potato chips and bake for another 10 minutes.
7. Let rest for 10 minutes before serving.

Serves 8

Finger-Licking Sandwiches

Burgers and Sandwiches

Breakfast

The Burger Is *Still* Better with Butter

In Sticky Fingers and Tenderloins I included the Burger Is Better with Butter recipe. After a year of developing burger recipes this is still my best one. The butter is what truly makes this burger delicious. So here it is again.

3 lb.	regular ground beef	1 tbsp.	Dijon mustard
1	onion, finely chopped	Pinch	cayenne pepper
3 cloves	garlic, minced		Salt and freshly ground
4 tbsp.	butter, softened		black pepper
1 tbsp.	chopped fresh parsley	6 or 12	burger buns
1 tbsp.	Worcestershire sauce	1/2 cup	melted butter

1. Preheat grill to medium-high.
2. In a large bowl, combine the beef, onion, garlic, 4 tbsp. butter, parsley, Worcestershire sauce, mustard, cayenne pepper, salt and black pepper.
3. Form into 12 equal-sized patties. (A flatter burger will cook more evenly and faster than a ball-like burger.)
4. Grill burgers for 4 to 5 minutes per side for medium-well.
5. Brush burger buns with melted butter and grill cut side down until crisp and golden brown.
6. Serve with your favorite burger garnishes. I like the works, and my list of the works is obscene.

Serves 6 or 12

The More Than Ultimate Burger Garnish List

Any of these items can be used on beef, chicken, turkey or fish burgers. Remember, there are no rules when building a better burger. Just use your imagination and have fun. Build a different burger with every grilling adventure.

Ketchup	
Mustard	(prepared, Dijon, Pommery, honey mustard or spicy)
Relish	(green, zucchini, tomato or corn)
Pickles	(sour dills, bread and butter, kosher or Spicy Garlic Dills, page 62)
Onions	(red, white, yellow; sweet or tart; raw, fried or grilled)
Salsa	
Cheese	(aged Cheddar, Swiss, Brie, Cambozola, mozzarella, blue, jalapeño Jack, Muenster, process, Camembert, goat cheese or provolone)
Peameal bacon	
Bacon	
Italian sausage patty	
Bratwurst sausage	
Fried egg	
Pickled egg	
Grilled Portobello mushrooms	
Lettuce	(green leaf, red leaf, iceberg, or romaine)
Tomato	(red, yellow or green as long they are fresh and full of flavor)
Peanut butter	

Grilled vegetables (peppers, mushrooms, onions, zucchini, eggplant and asparagus)

Blue cheese dressing
Ranch dressing
Caesar dressing
Sauerkraut
BBQ sauce
Mayonnaise
Steak sauce
Jalapeño peppers (fresh or pickled)
Pickled banana peppers
Sautéed mushrooms
Chili
Nacho cheese sauce
Avocado
Hot sauce
Oyster sauce
Grilled bologna
Grilled shrimp
Deep-fried breaded onion rings
Deep-fried breaded oysters
Deep-fried breaded clams
BBQ pulled pork (page 168)
Pickled beets
Hummus
Tzatziki
French onion dip
Anchovies
And the very best burger topping: The Stuff (page 74)

The Stuff

Many fast-food chains offer their own special toppings. McDonald's has its special sauce, In-N-Out Burger in California has Thousand Island dressing, and in my town of Toronto, Lick's has its Guk. I've created what I call the Stuff. It is all your burger needs instead of ketchup, mustard or relish.

Chipotle chilies in adobo can be found in many supermarkets or Mexican grocery stores. They add spice and a smoky flavor.

1	can (7 oz.) chipotle chilies in adobo sauce	1	lime, juiced
1¼ cups	sour cream	3	green onions, finely chopped
½ cup	cream cheese, softened	½ tsp.	salt
¼ cup	mayonnaise	¼ tsp.	coarsely ground black pepper
½ cup	shredded aged Cheddar cheese		

1. In a food processor, purée the chipotle chilies and adobo until smooth. Set aside 2 tbsp. and refrigerate or freeze the remainder for use in other recipes.
2. In the food processor, blend until smooth the 2 tbsp. chipotle purée, sour cream, cream cheese and mayonnaise.
3. Add the Cheddar, lime juice, green onions, salt and pepper. Pulse to just blend.
4. Adjust seasoning if necessary. Refrigerate for 1 hour before using.

Makes 2½ cups

The Hoser HAM-burger

Hey, this burger needs to be served with beer. I think that hosers Bob and Doug would be proud to call this burger Canadian, eh?

2 lb.	regular ground pork		1 tsp.	ground dried sage
1 lb.	1/4-inch-thick slices Black Forest ham or back bacon, diced		Pinch	cayenne pepper
				Salt to taste
1	onion, finely chopped		6 or 12	burger buns
4 cloves	garlic, minced		1/2 cup	melted butter
1/4 cup	Dijon mustard			
2 tbsp.	chopped fresh parsley			
2 tsp.	black pepper			
2 tsp.	crushed red chilies			

Garnishes

From the list, baby! Check the list! (page 73)

1. Preheat grill to medium-high.
2. In a large bowl, combine the ground pork, ham, onion, garlic, mustard, parsley, black pepper, crushed chilies, sage, cayenne pepper and salt.
3. Form into 12 equal-sized patties. (A flatter burger will cook more evenly and faster than a ball-like burger.)
4. Grill burgers for 4 to 5 minutes per side for medium-well.
5. Brush burger buns with melted butter and grill cut side down until crisp and golden brown.
6. I recommend garnishing these HAM-burgers with Swiss cheese, fresh tomatoes, lettuce, spicy mustard and grilled back bacon, eh?

Serves 6 or 12

Pamela's Three-Meat Burgers

My dearest Pamela makes some incredibly tasty burgers. She likes to make them really thin and cook them quickly so they are crispy on the outside and just done on the inside.

1 lb.	regular ground beef	1	small egg
1 lb.	ground veal	1 tbsp.	chopped fresh parsley
1 lb.	ground pork	2 tsp.	Worcestershire sauce
3 cloves	garlic, minced		Salt and pepper to taste
1	small onion, finely chopped	6 or 12	large burger buns
2	green onions, finely chopped	1/2 cup	melted butter

1. Preheat grill to medium-high.
2. In a large bowl, combine the beef, veal, pork, garlic, onion, green onions, egg, parsley, Worcestershire sauce, salt and pepper.
3. Form into 12 equal-sized patties. (A flatter burger will cook more evenly and faster than a ball-like burger.)
4. Grill burgers for 2 to 3 minutes per side for medium-well.
5. Brush burger buns with melted butter and grill cut side down until crisp and golden brown.
6. Serve with your favorite burger garnishes. I like to stack these burgers and add layers of cheese and grilled onions and mushrooms.

Serves 6 or 12

Christine's Bistro Burger Stuffed with Smoked Gruyère and Topped with Mashed Potatoes and Caramelized Red Onion Gravy

Beef, cheese, mashed potatoes and gravy all on one plate—it doesn't get much better than this. Christine is a decadent chef with a passion for great-tasting burgers. This is her favorite recipe.

3 lb.	ground sirloin	1 lb.	shredded smoked Gruyère cheese
2 cloves	garlic, minced		
1	small red onion, finely chopped	8	sourdough burger buns
		1/2 cup	melted butter
3 tbsp.	BBQ sauce		Goat Cheese Mashed Potatoes (page 64)
1 tbsp.	chopped fresh thyme		
	Salt and pepper to taste		Caramelized Red Onion Gravy (recipe follows)

1. In a large bowl, combine the sirloin, garlic, onion, BBQ sauce, thyme, salt and pepper.
2. Form into 16 equal-sized patties. (A flatter burger will cook more evenly and faster than a ball-like burger.)
3. Pressing firmly between your hands, shape the Gruyère cheese into 8 pucks a little smaller than the diameter of the patties.
4. Place a puck of cheese on 8 of the patties, cover with the remaining patties, and press the edges together to seal in the cheese. Cover and refrigerate for 1 hour to allow the meat to set.
5. Preheat grill to medium-high.
6. Grill burgers for 4 to 5 minutes per side for medium-well.
7. Brush burger buns with melted butter and grill cut side down until crisp and golden brown.

8. Place a stuffed burger on the bottom of each toasted bun. Top with a scoop of Goat Cheese Mashed Potatoes. Ladle Caramelized Red Onion Gravy over the potatoes and burger. Top with top half of bun.

9. Eat with a knife and fork.

Serves 8

Caramelized Red Onion Gravy

1/4 cup	butter		1 1/2 cups	beef stock
3	red onions, sliced		1/2 cup	red wine
4 cloves	garlic, minced		1/2 cup	steak sauce
1/4 cup	all-purpose flour			Salt and pepper
1 tbsp.	chopped fresh thyme			

1. In a medium saucepan, melt the butter over medium heat. Cook the onions and garlic, stirring occasionally, until the onions are tender and golden brown, 15 to 20 minutes.

2. Stir in the flour and thyme. Cook, stirring constantly, for 4 to 5 minutes, being careful not to burn the flour.

3. Add the beef stock 1/2 cup at a time, stirring constantly until smooth and thickened. Stir in the red wine and steak sauce. Reduce heat to low and simmer for 15 minutes, stirring occasionally.

4. Season to taste with salt and pepper. Keep warm until needed.

Makes about 2 1/2 cups

Portobello Mushroom Lamb Burgers

Portobello mushrooms are meaty and have a full-bodied flavor that blends perfectly with lamb. If you are not a fan of lamb, use ground sirloin instead.

4 large	Portobello mushroom caps, cleaned	2 tbsp.	chopped fresh rosemary
		1 tbsp.	Worcestershire sauce
1/4 cup	olive oil	2 tsp.	black pepper
1/4 cup	balsamic vinegar	2 tsp.	curry powder
	Salt and pepper to taste	1 tsp.	ground cumin
3 lb.	ground lamb	1/2 cup	goat cheese
6 cloves	garlic, minced	12	pocket-style pita breads
1	onion, diced	1 bunch	arugula
1/2 cup	golden raisins		Hummus, tzatziki or mayonnaise, for garnish
1/4 cup	grainy mustard		

1. In a large bowl, combine the Portobello mushroom caps, oil, vinegar, salt and pepper. Marinate for 2 to 4 hours.
2. Preheat grill to medium-high.
3. Remove mushroom caps from marinade and discard marinade. Grill mushroom caps until tender, 5 to 6 minutes per side. Let cool. Cut each mushroom cap in half and thinly slice each half crosswise.
4. In the bowl, combine lamb, garlic, onion, raisins, mustard, rosemary, Worcestershire sauce, pepper, curry powder, cumin and salt to taste. Fold in the mushrooms.
5. Form into 12 equal-sized patties. (A flatter burger will cook more evenly and faster than a ball-like burger.)
6. Grill burgers for 4 to 5 minutes per side for medium-well.
7. Top each burger with goat cheese and close lid for 1 minute or until cheese is soft.
8. Warm pita breads on grill. Cut 1 inch off one side of each pita and gently separate each side to form a pocket. Fill pocket with lamb burger and arugula and garnish with humus, tzatziki or mayonnaise.

Serves 6 or 12

Sassy BBQ Chicken Burgers

These burgers are not too hot and spicy, but if you want them that way, use a spicy BBQ sauce. Try this burger with ground turkey too.

2 lb.	ground chicken	1¼ cups	gourmet BBQ sauce
3	boneless, skinless chicken breasts (about 1 lb.), diced	¼ cup	coarse fresh bread crumbs
1	small red onion, finely chopped	1 tbsp.	Bone Dust BBQ Spice (page 99)
2 cloves	garlic, minced		Vegetable oil
1	jalapeño pepper, finely chopped	6 or 12	potato bread hamburger buns
			Whatever garnish you desire

1. Combine the ground chicken, diced chicken, onion, garlic, jalapeño, ¼ cup of the BBQ sauce, bread crumbs and Bone Dust BBQ Spice.
2. Form into 12 equal-sized patties. (A flatter burger will cook more evenly and faster than a ball-like burger.) Cover with plastic wrap and refrigerate for 2 hours to allow the burgers to set.
3. Preheat grill to medium-high.
4. Brush burgers with oil. Grill burgers, brushing each side with the remaining 1 cup of BBQ sauce, until the juices run clear and the burger is well done, 4 to 5 minutes per side.
5. Grill buns cut side down until toasted.
6. Serve burgers on buns. I like these loaded with pickled hot peppers, process cheese and bacon.

Serves 6 to 12

Screech Salmon Burgers

A little Newfoundland Screech rum will make anything taste delicious. Make sure to save a few shots of Screech for the chef.

Salmon burgers are delicate, so using a grill topper will make turning these burgers a lot easier.

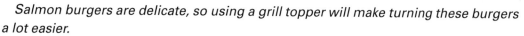

2 lb.	skinless Atlantic salmon fillets		Vegetable oil
1	egg white	4 to 8	egg buns or bagels
2	large shallots, finely chopped		**Garnishes**
2	green onions, finely chopped		Thinly sliced red onion
2 tbsp.	lemon juice		Softened cream cheese
2 tbsp.	Screech		Capers
1 tbsp.	chopped fresh dill		Mom's Tartar Sauce (recipe follows)
1 tbsp.	hot prepared horseradish		
1 tsp.	Bone Dust BBQ Spice (page 99)		

1. Cut the salmon into 1-inch pieces. Place salmon in a food processor and pulse until coarsely chopped and the salmon begins binding together. Transfer to a bowl.
2. Add the egg white, shallots, green onions, lemon juice, Screech, dill, horseradish and Bone Dust BBQ Spice. Combine well.
3. Form into 8 equal-sized patties. (A flatter burger will cook more evenly and faster than a ball-like burger.) Cover with plastic wrap and refrigerate for 2 hours to allow the burgers to set.
4. Preheat grill to medium-high.
5. Brush burgers with vegetable oil. Grill burgers for 4 to 5 minutes per side for medium-well. Grill buns until toasted.
6. Serve burgers on buns garnished with red onion, cream cheese, capers and a healthy dollop of tartar sauce.

Serves 4 to 8

Mom's Tartar Sauce

Got to love your mom!

1¹/₂ cups	mayonnaise	1 tbsp.	lemon juice
¹/₂ cup	zucchini relish		Salt and pepper

1. In a bowl, whisk together the mayonnaise, relish and lemon juice. Season to taste with salt and pepper. Cover and refrigerate. Sauce keeps, refrigerated, for up to 2 weeks.

Makes approximately 2 cups

Grilled Vegetable Burgers

Over the last year or so I have had numerous requests for low-fat or vegetarian recipes. This is a new avenue for me, but I think you will enjoy this tasty veggie burger.

2 tbsp.	olive oil		1/4 cup	grated Parmesan cheese
4 cloves	garlic, minced		1/4 cup	pine nuts, coarsely chopped
1	red onion, diced		1 tbsp.	chopped fresh basil
8	shiitake mushrooms, thinly sliced		1 tbsp.	balsamic vinegar
1	red bell pepper, diced		1/4 to 1/2 cup	fresh bread crumbs
1	jalapeño pepper, finely chopped			Cayenne pepper
				Salt and pepper
1 cup	corn kernels (thawed if frozen)		8 balls	bocconcini cheese, each cut into 4 or 5 slices
1 cup	green peas (thawed if frozen)		8	hamburger buns
1 1/4 cups	tomato sauce			Sliced vine-ripened tomatoes and alfalfa sprouts, for garnish
1	can (14 oz.) chick peas, drained, rinsed and mashed			

1. Heat the oil in a large nonstick frying pan over medium heat. Sauté the garlic, onion and mushrooms until tender, 3 to 5 minutes. Stir in the red pepper, jalapeño, corn and green peas; cook until hot, 3 to 5 more minutes. Remove from heat and let cool.
2. Stir in 1/4 cup of the tomato sauce, chick peas, Parmesan, pine nuts, basil, vinegar and enough bread crumbs to bind mixture firmly. Season with cayenne, salt and pepper.
3. Form into 8 equal-sized patties. Cover and refrigerate for 2 hours to set.
4. Preheat grill to medium. Spray a grill topper with nonstick cooking spray.
5. Spray the burgers with nonstick cooking spray. Grill burgers on topper until golden brown and heated through, 4 to 5 minutes per side.
6. Top with remaining 1 cup tomato sauce and slices of bocconcini. Close lid and cook burgers for 1 minute or until the cheese has melted.
7. Lightly toast buns. Serve burgers on buns with tomatoes and alfalfa sprouts.

Serves 8

Grilled Tuna and Vegetable Pan Bagnat

My version of this classic French sandwich is made with all of the vegetables and the tuna being grilled first. Use a grilling basket to make grilling the vegetables a lot easier. This is one big sandwich—and it's perfect for a picnic.

1	red onion, sliced			Salt and pepper
1	zucchini, halved and sliced crosswise		2	tuna steaks (each about 6 oz. and 1 inch thick)
1	red bell pepper, cut into wedges		3 cloves	garlic, minced
1	yellow bell pepper, cut into wedges		4	anchovy fillets, minced
1	green bell pepper, cut into wedges		1/4 cup	chopped fresh basil
8	jumbo white mushrooms, sliced 1/4 inch thick		2 tbsp.	Dijon mustard
1 bunch	asparagus, trimmed		1/2 cup	sliced black olives
1/2 cup	olive oil		1/4 cup	drained capers
1/2 cup	red wine vinegar		1	baguette (about 18 inches long)
			2	vine-ripened tomatoes, thinly sliced
			2 cups	mixed baby greens

1. Preheat grill to medium-high.
2. In a large bowl, combine the onion, zucchini, bell peppers, mushrooms, asparagus, 1/4 cup of the olive oil and 1/4 cup of the vinegar; toss well. Season to taste with salt and pepper.
3. Place vegetables in a grill basket and grill until slightly charred and tender, 5 to 6 minutes per side. Transfer vegetables to a bowl and let cool.
4. Meanwhile, season tuna steaks with salt, pepper and a little olive oil. Grill for 2 to 3 minutes per side for medium-rare. Let cool.
5. In a bowl, whisk together the remaining 1/4 cup of olive oil and vinegar, the garlic, anchovies, basil and mustard. Season the dressing to taste with salt and pepper.
6. Drain the grilled vegetables. Add the olives, capers and dressing. Toss gently.
7. Cut the tuna steaks into 1/4-inch-thick slices.

8. Cut the baguette in half lengthwise. Arrange the grilled vegetable mixture evenly over the bottom half of the baguette. Top with layers of tuna, tomatoes and the salad greens. Top with the top half of the baguette. Wrap tightly in plastic wrap and refrigerate for 1 hour for flavors to blend.

9. Unwrap the sandwich and, using a sharp serrated knife, slice the sandwich into 4 or 8 pieces. Serve immediately or wrap pieces individually for a picnic.

Serves 4

Grilled Philly Cheese Steak Sandwiches

Cube steak is an inexpensive cut of beef that has been tenderized.

4	cube steaks (each 4 oz.)		1	poblano pepper, seeded and thinly sliced
4 cloves	garlic, minced		2 tbsp.	olive oil
1/4 cup	soy sauce		1 tsp.	ground fennel
2 tbsp.	brown sugar		1/2 tsp.	cayenne pepper
2 tbsp.	Worcestershire sauce			Salt and pepper to taste
1 tbsp.	cracked black pepper		4 slices	provolone cheese
1	large red onion, sliced		4 slices	mozzarella cheese
4	jumbo white mushrooms, thickly sliced		4 slices	Swiss cheese
1	green bell pepper, cut into 1/4-inch slices		4	6-inch hoagie buns, halved crosswise
1	red bell pepper, cut into 1/4-inch slices		2 tbsp.	melted butter
			4 tsp.	mayonnaise

1. In a glass dish large enough to hold the steaks in one layer, whisk together the garlic, soy sauce, sugar, Worcestershire sauce and black pepper. Add steaks, turning to coat. Marinate, covered and refrigerated, for 4 hours.
2. Meanwhile, in a large bowl, toss together the onion, mushrooms, green pepper, red pepper, poblano pepper, oil, fennel, cayenne pepper, salt and black pepper.
3. Once the meat has marinated, preheat grill to high.
4. Grill the vegetables in a grill basket until lightly charred and tender, 8 to 12 minutes per side. Transfer to a bowl and adjust seasoning.
5. Grill steak for 2 to 3 minutes per side for medium doneness. Top steaks with the vegetable mixture. Top with slices of provolone, mozzarella and Swiss cheese. Close the lid and cook for 1 to 2 minutes or until the cheese melts.
6. Brush buns with melted butter and grill until golden brown and crisp. Top each bun with a cheese steak, drizzle with mayonnaise and top with the top of the bun.
7. Serve immediately with a side of BBQ sauce.

Makes 4 sandwiches

Grilled Halibut Fishwich

Halibut is a most delicious fish: rich with flavor, tender and delicious. When I'm in the mood for deep-fried halibut I usually go to Chubby's Fish and Chips Restaurant on Islington Avenue in Toronto. It's awesome. When I'm in the mood for something lighter, I make this grilled sandwich.

4	fresh skinless halibut fillets (each 4 oz.)		Salt and pepper to taste
2 tbsp.	Bay Seasoning (page 101)	1/4 cup	melted butter
2 tbsp.	vegetable oil	8 slices	sourdough bread
4 cloves	garlic, minced	4 leaves	green leaf lettuce
1/4 cup	lemon juice	2 cups	Tropical Coleslaw (page 19)
1/4 cup	Dijon mustard		Ted's Tartar Sauce (recipe follows)
2 tbsp.	chopped fresh thyme		

1. Season halibut with Bay Seasoning, pressing the seasoning into the flesh. Brush halibut with oil.
2. In a glass dish large enough to hold the halibut in one layer, whisk together the garlic, lemon juice, mustard, thyme, salt and pepper. Add halibut, turning to coat, and marinate, covered, for 30 minutes.
3. Preheat grill to medium-high.
4. Grill halibut, basting with melted butter, until just cooked through and lightly charred, 3 to 4 minutes per side.
5. Grill bread until slightly crisp. Butter the bread. Top 4 slices of bread with halibut. Top with leaf lettuce and coleslaw. Top with the remaining slices of bread.
6. Serve immediately with my tartar sauce. (I like my Mom's on page 82, but mine just works better for this sandwich.)

Makes 4 sandwiches

Ted's Tartar Sauce

1	dill pickle, finely chopped	2 tbsp.	chopped capers
1	small shallot, diced	1 tbsp.	lemon juice
1	green onion, chopped		Cayenne pepper
1 cup	mayonnaise		Salt and pepper

1. In a bowl, stir together the pickle, shallot, green onion, mayonnaise, capers and lemon juice. Season to taste with cayenne, salt and pepper.

Makes about 1 cup

Smoked Chicken Wings, p. 47

Portobello Mushrooms Stuffed with BBQ Pulled Pork, p. 38

Cedar-Planked Salmon with Crab and Scallop Crust, p. 202

Grilled Bacon-Wrapped Bananas with Bourbon Honey Sauce and Smoked Chocolate Crème Fraîche Ice Cream, pp. 218 and 225

BBQ Breakfast Pepper Baked Eggs

Back in 1997, while promoting my TV show Cottage Country, *I went on air with Magic 100 Radio in Ottawa. I needed to do a funky breakfast on the grill, and this is what I came up with. A few years later I prepared this recipe for the folks at* Canada AM *and it was a hit. So now its time to share it with you.*

4	large red or yellow bell peppers	1 tbsp.	chopped fresh thyme
1	large red onion	8	large eggs
8	large shiitake mushrooms		Freshly ground black pepper to taste
2 tbsp.	olive oil	1 cup	shredded Cheddar cheese
2 tsp.	Bone Dust BBQ Spice (page 99)		

1. Preheat grill to medium-high.
2. Cut the bell peppers in half through the stem. Carefully remove the seeds and ribs. Set peppers aside.
3. Slice the onion into rounds. Toss onions with the mushrooms, oil and Bone Dust BBQ Spice.
4. Grill the onions and mushrooms in a grill basket until slightly charred and tender, about 10 minutes.
5. Dice the onions and mushrooms. Place in a bowl and toss with the thyme.
6. Grill the peppers, turning twice, until they just start to get soft, about 5 minutes.
7. Transfer the peppers, cut side up, to a grill topper. Place 2 tbsp. of the mushroom mixture in each pepper. Crack an egg into each pepper. Grill peppers with the lid closed for 5 minutes. Top eggs with the Cheddar cheese. Close lid and bake for 3 more minutes or until the cheese melts.
8. Serve with grilled peameal bacon steaks, grilled toast and a breakfast shake.

Serves 8

Cast-Iron Breakfast Strata

This wonderful breakfast egg pudding can be prepared the night before and baked on the grill in the morning. You can also add cooked bacon when you add the cheese.

4 tbsp.	vegetable oil	8	day-old croissants
1	large onion, thinly sliced	2 cups	shredded aged white Cheddar cheese
2 cups	sliced mushrooms		
2 tbsp.	chopped fresh herbs	12	large eggs
	Salt and pepper to taste	1 1/2 cups	heavy cream

1. In a large frying pan, heat 2 tbsp. of the oil over high heat. Sauté the onion until tender and slightly caramelized, 5 to 7 minutes. Add the mushrooms; cook, stirring frequently, until the mushrooms are tender and all of the liquid has evaporated. Stir in the herbs, salt and pepper. Let cool.
2. Tear the croissants into 2-inch cubes. In a large bowl, combine the croissants, mushroom mixture and Cheddar cheese. Gently mix and season to taste with salt and pepper.
3. Brush a large, deep cast-iron pan with the remaining 2 tbsp. oil. Transfer the croissant mixture to the cast-iron pan.
4. In another bowl, whisk together the eggs and cream. Season to taste with salt and pepper. Pour the mixture over the croissants, filling to the edge of the pan. (Depending on the size of your pan, you may need to add an extra egg and a little more cream.) Gently push all of the croissant mixture down into the egg mixture. Cover with plastic wrap and refrigerate overnight.
5. Preheat grill to medium-high.
6. Remove plastic wrap from the strata and cover loosely with foil. Place on the grill, close the lid and bake for 45 minutes. Remove the foil, close the lid and cook for another 15 minutes or until the top has puffed and browned. A wooden skewer inserted in the middle should come out clean and dry.
7. Carefully remove from grill and let sit for 10 minutes before serving.

Serves 6 to 8

Mucked-Up Eggs

My Dad used to make this breakfast for me as a kid. The definition of a mucked-up egg is 2 soft-boiled eggs spooned over diced buttered toast and then mucked up with a spoon. Here's my updated version of this classic family recipe.

3 tbsp.	butter	8 slices	bacon, cut in 1/2-inch pieces
1	small onion, diced		Salt, black pepper and
2 cups	halved button mushrooms		cayenne pepper to taste
2	green onions, chopped	6 thick slices	white bread
1 tbsp.	chopped fresh parsley	8	large eggs
1 tbsp.	honey mustard		Hot sauce

1. Melt the butter in a large frying pan over medium-high heat. Cook the onion and mushrooms, stirring occasionally, until golden brown, 10 to 12 minutes. Transfer to a bowl and toss with green onions, parsley and honey mustard.
2. In the same pan, fry the bacon until crisp. Add to mushroom mixture and season with salt, black pepper and cayenne pepper. Remove from heat and keep warm.
3. Toast the bread. Butter the bread and cut into 1/2-inch cubes. Toss with the mushroom mixture.
4. Soft-boil the eggs for 3 minutes.
5. Spoon equal amounts of the mushroom mixture into 4 wide-mouthed beer glasses.
6. Carefully peel the eggs and spoon 1 egg into each glass. Season to taste with salt, pepper and hot sauce and stir until mucked up.

Serves 4

Breakfast Grilled Steak and Eggs

Here's a lumberjack breakfast treat for those days when you wake up screaming hungry. If it's a weekend, have a beer with this hearty breakfast.

4	beef tenderloin steaks (each 8 oz.)	1	large red bell pepper, thinly sliced
1/4 cup + 1 tbsp.	Hell's Fire Chili Paste (page 102)	2 cups	sliced shiitake mushrooms
		1 tsp.	chopped fresh sage
			Salt and pepper
2 tbsp.	butter	1 lb.	breakfast sausages
1	large Spanish onion, sliced	4	extra-large eggs

1. Rub steaks with 1/4 cup of the Chili Paste. Marinate, covered and refrigerated, for at least 2 hours or overnight.
2. Melt butter in a large frying pan over medium-high heat. Sauté onion, red pepper and mushrooms until golden brown and tender, 8 to 10 minutes. Stir in the remaining 1 tbsp. Chili Paste, the sage, and salt and pepper to taste. Remove from heat and keep warm.
3. Preheat grill to medium.
4. Grill sausages until fully cooked and crispy, 8 to 10 minutes. Set aside sausages, loosely covered with foil.
5. Grill steaks for 3 to 5 minutes per side for medium-rare. Set aside steaks, loosely covered with foil.
6. On the grill side burner (or on the stove), fry the eggs in a little butter or oil.
7. Put steaks on plates and top each steak with mushroom mixture. Top with sausages and top with a fried egg.
8. Serve with a cold beer.

Serves 4

The Muffin for Breakfast and Lunch

Fruit-flavored muffins are pretty good, but personally I believe that muffins should be loaded with bacon, cheese and other good stuff. Try these savory muffins on for size! They're awesome served with poached eggs or a steak.

8 slices	thick-cut bacon, diced	2	green onions, finely chopped
4¹/₂ cups	all-purpose flour	1 cup	¹/₄-inch cubes Cheddar cheese
4 tsp.	baking powder		
1¹/₂ tsp.	salt	1 cup	¹/₄-inch cubes Swiss cheese
2	large eggs	1 tbsp.	chopped fresh parsley
2 cups	whole milk	Pinch	cayenne pepper
¹/₂ cup	melted butter		

1. Fry the bacon until crisp; set aside to drain on paper towels. Set aside 1 tbsp. of the bacon fat.
2. Preheat oven to 425°F. Grease a muffin pan.
3. In a large bowl, sift together the flour, baking powder and salt.
4. In a separate bowl, beat together the eggs, milk, butter and reserved bacon fat. Pour into the flour mixture; stir quickly to mix completely. Gently fold in the bacon, green onions, Cheddar cheese, Swiss cheese, parsley and cayenne.
5. Spoon into muffin tins, filling to the top. Bake until golden brown and the cheese is bubbling, 18 to 25 minutes.

Makes 12 really big muffins

Seasoning
Rubs and
Pastes

Malabar Pepper Rub

The Malabar coast of India is best known for its black pepper. This rub is a variation of one I discovered on an expedition to Cochin, India. This is a great rub for beef, chicken and salmon.

¼ cup	cracked black peppercorns	2 tbsp.	granulated onion
¼ cup	crushed red chilies	1 tbsp.	sugar
¼ cup	coarse kosher salt	1 tbsp.	curry powder
2 tbsp.	granulated garlic	1 tbsp.	ground coriander

1. In a bowl mix together the black peppercorns, crushed red chilies, salt, garlic, onion, sugar, curry powder and coriander.
2. Store in an airtight container in a cool, dry place away from heat and light.

Makes about 1¼ cups

Smoked Garlic

Roasted Garlic has a natural sweetness that adds wonderful flavor to many dishes, but smoked garlic is something else!

8 large heads garlic	Hickory smoking chips, soaked in cold water

1. Prepare smoker as per manufacturer's instructions to a temperature of 225°F.
2. Using a sharp knife cut the top off each head of garlic, exposing the cloves.
3. Place garlic heads cut side down on the top rack of the smoker and close the lid. Smoke garlic for approximately 3 hours, until tender and golden brown.
4. Remove garlic from smoker and carefully peel the skin from the cloves of garlic.

Gilroy Roasted Garlic Paste

Not all rubs are dry rubs. This paste recipe uses lots of freshly roasted garlic. I remember the first time that I drove through the town of Gilroy, California. Even though my car windows were up, the smell of fresh garlic was so thick in the air that it easily filled the car.
Rub this paste liberally into chicken, lamb or beef.

3 large heads	garlic	2 tbsp.	coarsely ground black pepper
1/2 cup	(approx.) olive oil	1 tbsp.	coarse kosher salt
1/4 cup	grainy mustard	1 tbsp.	balsamic vinegar
2 tbsp.	chopped fresh parsley		
2 tbsp.	chopped fresh rosemary		

1. Preheat oven to 325°F.
2. Separate the cloves of garlic and peel them. Place in an ovenproof dish just large enough to hold them. Pour enough olive oil over the garlic to cover the cloves.
3. Roast garlic for 30 to 45 minutes or until golden brown and tender. Let cool in the oil.
4. In a food processor, place the roasted garlic, 1/2 cup of the reserved olive oil, the mustard, parsley, rosemary, pepper, salt and vinegar. Blend until smooth.
5. Store in a sealed container, refrigerated, for up to 2 weeks.

Makes about 2 cups

Great Canadian Steak Spice (a.k.a. Montreal Steak Spice)

This has got to be the best rub for steaks. I believe that the saltier the rub, the better the steak will be.

1/2 cup	coarse kosher salt	1/4 cup	cracked coriander seeds
1/4 cup	coarsely ground black pepper	1/4 cup	granulated garlic
		1/4 cup	granulated onion
1/4 cup	coarsely ground white pepper	1/4 cup	crushed red chilies
1/4 cup	mustard seeds	1/4 cup	dill seed

1. Combine the salt, black pepper, white pepper, mustard seeds, coriander seeds, garlic, onion, crushed chilies and dill seed.
2. Store in an airtight container in a cool, dry place away from heat and light.

Makes 2 1/2 cups

Bone Dust BBQ Spice (a.k.a. The Best BBQ Rub)

As you may well know, I love to grill. Well, this is my favorite recipe for a BBQ spice. It is from my Sticks and Stones *cookbook. It just doesn't get any better than this one.*

1/2 cup	paprika	2 tbsp.	hot dry mustard
1/4 cup	chili powder	1 tbsp.	black pepper
3 tbsp.	salt	1 tbsp.	dried basil
2 tbsp.	ground coriander	1 tbsp.	dried thyme
2 tbsp.	garlic powder	1 tbsp.	ground cumin
2 tbsp.	sugar	1 tbsp.	cayenne pepper
2 tbsp.	curry powder		

1. Mix together the paprika, chili powder, salt, coriander, garlic powder, sugar, curry powder, dry mustard, black pepper, basil, thyme, cumin and cayenne.
2. Store in an airtight container in a cool, dry place away from heat and light.

Makes about 2 1/2 cups

Salmon Seasoning

I love salmon. I think growing up with a Newfie dad had something to do with this. Here's a tasty seasoning that blends nicely with the richness of salmon.

1/4 cup	lemon pepper	1 tbsp.	paprika
1/4 cup	coarse kosher salt	1 tbsp.	granulated garlic
1/4 cup	dill seed	1 tbsp.	granulated onion
1/4 cup	dried coriander	2 tsp.	cayenne pepper
2 tbsp.	dried dill	2 tsp.	sugar

1. Combine the lemon pepper, salt, dill seed, coriander, dill, paprika, garlic, onion, cayenne and sugar.
2. Store in an airtight container in a cool, dry place away from heat and light.

Makes about 1 1/2 cups

Bay Seasoning

Inspired by the countless days I spent crabbing on Chesapeake Bay, here is a classic seasoning for crab boils, shrimp boils and clam bakes. The most famous of its kind is Old Bay Seasoning, a truly excellent seasoning. I think mine is just a little better, of course, but if you don't have the time to prepare this recipe by all means use Old Bay.

1/2 cup	paprika	1/4 cup	garlic powder
1/4 cup	celery salt	1/4 cup	onion powder
1/4 cup	coarse kosher salt	1/4 cup	ground coriander
1/4 cup	cayenne pepper	1/4 cup	ground cumin
1/4 cup	ground black pepper	2 tbsp.	sugar
1/4 cup	ground white pepper	1 tbsp.	curry powder

1. Combine the paprika, celery salt, salt, cayenne, black pepper, white pepper, garlic powder, onion powder, coriander, cumin, sugar and curry powder.
2. Store in an airtight container in a cool, dry place away from heat and light.

Makes about 3 cups

Hell's Fire Chili Paste

Some folks just like it to be insanely hot. So here it is. Blow your brains out with this rubbing paste. Good luck, and remember to keep lots of water on hand. Also, you may want to use rubber gloves and a mask when preparing this.

1	can (7 oz.) smoked chipotle chilies	2	limes, juiced
6	habanero peppers	1/4 cup	chopped fresh cilantro
3	green onions, coarsely chopped	1/4 cup	olive oil
4 cloves	garlic	1 tbsp.	sugar
		2 tsp.	salt

1. In a food processor, combine the chipotle chilies, habanero peppers, green onions, garlic, lime juice, cilantro, olive oil, sugar and salt. Blend until smooth.
2. Transfer to a small dish. Cover and refrigerate. Keeps for up to 2 weeks.

Makes about 1 1/2 cups

Mocha Coffee Rub

I love the flavor of coffee, and it has a wonderful affinity with beef and lamb.
*   I don't recommend using a coffee grinder here because the coffee needs to be*
coarse, not finely ground.

1/2 cup	mocha-flavored coffee beans	1/4 cup	olive oil
6 cloves	garlic, minced	2 tbsp.	molasses
1/4 cup	chopped fresh rosemary	2 tbsp.	balsamic vinegar
1/4 cup	chopped fresh parsley		Salt to taste
1/4 cup	cracked black pepper		

1. Using the bottom of a heavy frying pan, crush the coffee beans.
2. Stir together the crushed coffee beans, garlic, rosemary, parsley, pepper, olive oil, molasses, vinegar and salt.
3. Store, refrigerated, in a sealed container. Keeps up to 2 weeks.

Makes about 2 cups

Herb Mustard Rub

I love to use fresh herbs whenever possible. This combination of fresh herbs and mustard is a great way to enhance poultry and pork.

6 cloves	garlic, minced	1/4 cup	olive oil
1 cup	chopped fresh herbs (any combination of parsley, sage, rosemary, thyme, tarragon, dill and savory)	2 tbsp.	honey
		2 tbsp.	white wine vinegar
		1 tbsp.	coarsely ground black pepper
1/4 cup	Dijon mustard		Salt to taste
1/4 cup	grainy mustard		

1. Combine the garlic, herbs, Dijon mustard, grainy mustard, olive oil, honey, vinegar, pepper and salt.
2. Store, refrigerated, in a sealed container. Keeps up to 2 weeks.

Makes about 2 cups

Indonesian Cinnamon Rub

Cinnamon adds a natural sweetness to certain foods. It is not just for baking but is an excellent addition to many savory dishes.
This rub can be used on chicken, lamb and pork.

1/4 cup	cinnamon	1 tbsp.	ground cloves
2 tbsp.	sugar	1 tbsp.	ground ginger
2 tbsp.	ground cumin	1 tbsp.	garlic powder
2 tbsp.	ground allspice	1 tbsp.	salt

1. Combine the cinnamon, sugar, cumin, allspice, cloves, ginger, garlic powder and salt.
2. Store in an airtight container in a cool, dry place away from heat and light.

Makes about 1 cup

Jamaican Jerk Paste

This great recipe has been handed down to my dear friend Bridget from her family in Jamaica. It brings out the zing in any dish. The name "jerk" can only be attributed to the sudden rush your palate feels when eating it.

Jerk is a great seasoning for pork and chicken.

4	habanero or Scotch bonnet peppers	1/4 cup	olive oil
6	green onions, coarsely chopped	1/4 cup	lemon juice
		2 tbsp.	ground allspice
1/4 cup	water	2 tsp.	salt
1 cup	fresh cilantro leaves	1 tsp.	ground cloves
1 cup	fresh parsley leaves	1 tsp.	ground cumin
6 cloves	garlic	1 tsp.	black pepper

1. In a food processor or blender, purée the habanero peppers, green onions and water. Add the cilantro, parsley and garlic; purée until smooth. Add the olive oil, lemon juice, allspice, salt, cloves, cumin and black pepper. Blend until fully incorporated.
2. Store in a sealed container, refrigerated. Keeps up to 2 weeks.

Makes about 3 cups

Miami Spice Love Paste

Try this sweet and spicy rub on fish, shellfish, chicken or ribs.

6 cloves	garlic	1/4 cup	chopped fresh ginger
2	red finger chili peppers	1/4 cup	olive oil
4	green onions, coarsely chopped	1/4 cup	Grand Marnier
2 tbsp.	orange zest	2 tsp.	salt
1/2 cup	orange juice	2 tsp.	ground fennel
1/2 cup	fresh cilantro leaves	1 tsp.	cinnamon
		1 tsp.	black pepper

1. In a food processor or blender, combine the garlic, chili peppers, green onions, orange zest, orange juice, cilantro, ginger, olive oil, Grand Marnier, salt, fennel, cinnamon and black pepper. Blend until smooth.
2. Store, refrigerated, in a sealed container. Keeps up to 2 weeks.

Makes about 2 cups

Licorice Rub

Toasting spices extracts their natural oils, which brings out more flavor in your recipes. Use this rub on chicken and lamb.

4	star anise, broken into pieces	1/4 cup	black peppercorns
3	3-inch cinnamon sticks, broken into small pieces	1 tsp.	whole cloves
		1 tbsp.	granulated garlic
1/2 cup	fennel seeds	1 tbsp.	ground ginger
		1 tbsp.	salt

1. Heat a frying pan over medium heat. Toast the star anise, cinnamon sticks, fennel, peppercorns and whole cloves, stirring, until lightly toasted and fragrant, 3 to 5 minutes.
2. Using a spice/coffee mill, grind the spices into a fine powder. In a bowl, stir together the ground spices, garlic, ginger and salt.
3. Store in an airtight container in a cool, dry place away from heat and light.

Makes about 3/4 cup

RED-RUM Rub

This is a fiery paste ("red-rum" spelled backwards is...) that will make you blush.

8	red finger chili peppers	1/4 cup	red paprika
1	small red onion, quartered	1/4 cup	amber rum
1	red bell pepper, quartered	2 tsp.	red cayenne pepper
8 cloves	garlic	1 tsp.	salt
1/2 cup	red chili oil		

1. Preheat oven to 375°F.
2. In an ovenproof dish, toss together the red finger chili peppers, red onion, red bell pepper, garlic and red chili oil. Roast until all is very lightly charred and tender, 30 to 45 minutes.
3. In a food processor or blender, purée the mixture until smooth. Add the red paprika, rum, red cayenne pepper and salt. Pulse until incorporated.
4. Store, refrigerated, in a sealed container. Keeps up to 2 weeks.

Makes about 2 cups

Hot and Sticky Ribs

Beef Ribs

Buffalo Ribs

Lamb Ribs

Rib Types

Pork Baby Back Ribs

Baby back ribs are the ultimate rib. Cut from the loin, they are much leaner than spareribs and tend to have a higher meat-to-bone ratio. When prepared properly, these ribs provide the best eating. I recall once organizing the SkyDome Ribfest, a promotion for Loblaws Grocery Stores, during which we cooked a million pounds of baby back ribs.

Whether the ribs are fresh or frozen, look for ribs that have more loin meat attached. A baby back rib should weigh between 1¼ and 2 lb. Baby back ribs are more expensive than spareribs but are the best quality. As the saying goes, "You get what you pay for."

Pork Spareribs

Spareribs are cut from the side, or underbelly, of the pig. These ribs are quite meaty but are also fattier than baby back ribs. Weighing usually between 2½ and 3½ lb., these ribs can serve several people. Spareribs are usually sold with the soft bone brisket attached. This cartilage material is tough and fatty and is best trimmed off and used in soup stocks. Ask your butcher to remove the brisket for you.

The term "St. Louis rib" means that the soft bone brisket has been removed, which produces a rib that is more uniform in size and makes for easier cooking and eating. These ribs usually weigh around 2 lb.

Country-Style Pork Ribs

Country-style pork ribs are extremely meaty. In fact, there are usually just a few small bones attached. These ribs come from the rib end of the pork loin and are loaded with meat. They're priced less than baby back ribs and spareribs. These ribs require a little longer cooking time to ensure tenderness but are well worth the wait.

Pork Back Rib Tail Pieces

I was involved in developing a product for President's Choice called If Pigs Could Fly. This was a frozen appetizer that used a byproduct of the pork baby back rib. When the butcher prepares pork baby back ribs, the small "tail" piece must be removed from the end of the rib. Tail pieces are approximately 6 to 8 inches long and have small flat bones. They are to pork what the wing is to chicken—a great snack food.

Rib tail pieces are not always available and are best ordered through your favorite butcher. Allow at least 4 to 6 pieces per person.

Pork Shoulder

A whole pork shoulder consists of the blade bone, shank and foreleg and weighs approximately

15 to 20 lb. This is a lot of meat, and unless you are feeding a crowd of people and have a lot of time on your hands I do not recommend purchasing a whole shoulder. The whole shoulder is used in BBQ competitions.

You can find at your local butcher or grocery store smaller cuts from the shoulder area. The picnic roast (a.k.a. shoulder roast or Boston butt) is a smaller cut (approximately 5 to 7 lb.) and easier to prepare. The best method for preparation is to slowly smoke the shoulder pieces over low heat. Low and slow makes for succulent and tender.

Beef Ribs

These are enormous ribs that are cut from the loin of beef. They are best ordered from your favorite butcher, since most grocery stores do not carry them. They're usually bought up by the food service industry, which does not leave too many ribs for the retailer. As a chef at the SkyDome, I prepared many prime ribs of beef for our customers. I would often remove the back ribs after the beef was cooked and then grill the ribs and baste them generously with a smoky BBQ sauce. These ribs never made it to the customer, as I would serve them to my staff as a dinner treat.

"Monster Bones" or "Dinosaur Ribs," as they are frequently referred to on menus, are succulent and meaty. Have a lot of napkins on hand because the only true way to eat these is with your hands.

Beef Short Ribs

This inexpensive cut of meat is readily available in grocery stores. It is cut from the belly plate, or the chuck areas, of a steer and is composed of layers of meat, fat and flat rib bones. The fat cap of a short rib should be trimmed before cooking. These ribs are quite chunky and take a fair amount of time to cook.

You may also purchase what are called Maui or Miami ribs, depending where you are from. These ribs are cut approximately 1/2 inch thick across the short ribs. They have 4 or 5 bones in each and can be prepared quickly on the grill once they are marinated.

Lamb Ribs

Lamb ribs are popular in South Africa, Australia and the South Pacific but are not as well known to North American barbecue aficionados. Lamb ribs are smaller than pork ribs, weighing in at just around a pound. Lamb ribs have a thick fat cap, which should be removed before cooking. There is not a lot of meat on lamb ribs, so allow 2 racks per person. If you are a lover of lamb, then these ribs will make you really smile.

Cooking Methods

Boiling

Some chefs say never to boil ribs. I believe that you can—but make sure that you add some kind of flavoring to the water. Boiling ribs tends to remove the flavor and succulence from the meat, so you need to add something to replace the lost flavor, such as apple cider, pineapple juice, beer, ginger ale or stock. Boiling is not my favorite method of cooking ribs, but it does tenderize them. I would recommend boiling only pork spareribs and never boiling beef or lamb ribs.

Cooking Time: Cooking liquid temperature 210°F.
Allow approximately 30 minutes per lb.

2 to 3 lb. spareribs	90 minutes
1 to 2 lb. back ribs	60 minutes

Steaming

My friend Dave Nichol swears by steaming for cooking tender pork ribs. I agree with him. Steaming ribs allows the meat to tenderize without losing its flavor to the water, as in boiling. A large steamer pot will do the job. Flavor the steaming liquid with garlic, onions and assorted herbs and spices before steaming the ribs. Never steam beef ribs.

Cooking Time: Bring cooking liquid to a boil. Place steamer insert in pot and add ribs. Allow approximately 30 minutes per lb.

2 to 3 lb. spareribs	90 minutes
1 to 2 lb. back ribs	60 minutes
1 lb. lamb ribs	45 minutes

Oven Roasting

Oven roasting is a great way to cook ribs. This method suits all types of ribs (pork, beef and lamb). When preparing ribs for roasting, always rub them with a BBQ seasoning of some flavor. (See chapter 6 for rubs.) Preheat your oven to 350°F and place seasoned ribs on a wire rack in a roasting pan.

Cooking Time: Preheated 350°F oven.

2 to 3 lb. spareribs and beef ribs	75 to 90 minutes
1 to 2 lb. back rib and country-style ribs	60 to 75 minutes
1 lb. lamb ribs	45 to 60 minutes

Grilling

In this method of cooking, ribs are cooked fully on the grill, whereas boiling, steaming, roasting, smoking and braising all require that you finish the ribs on a hot grill before serving.

Grilling ribs requires low heat, patience and desire. These three "ingredients" will produce a great-tasting rib. Grilling is best suited for pork back and spareribs. The temperature of your grill should remain at around 325°F. Since cooking on a grill is with dry heat, you need to have some moisture to keep the ribs from drying out. Place a small pan of water in the bottom of the grill among the coals or on top of the grill bars. Marinate your ribs for 4 to 6 hours and then rub them with your favorite BBQ seasoning. Place them on the grill meaty side up, close the lid and cook the ribs until the meat is tender. Near the end of the cooking brush the ribs with your favorite BBQ sauce.

Cooking Time:	Preheated 325°F grill.	
	2 to 3 lb. spareribs and beef ribs	90 minutes
	1 to 2 lb. pork back ribs and country-style ribs	75 minutes
	1 lb. lamb ribs	60 minutes

Smoking

Smoking ribs—or real barbecue—is as much an art form as it is a method of cooking. Various styles of smokers are available for backyard use. Whatever kind you use, three basic principles apply. They're the same three principles of grilling ribs (see above) but with a few changes. Low heat is a must—around 200 to 225°F. You must have more patience (smoking can take anywhere from 3 to 7 hours, depending on the size and cut of your meat), and your desire will grow. So sit back, relax, crack a cold one and tend to your ribs.

For best results, use a charcoal smoker. You can smoke on a gas grill, but true lovers of barbecue smoke only over coals with flavored wood chips. Heat a small amount of charcoal to between 200 and 225°F.

Soak smoking chips in water for at least 1 hour before adding to hot coals. You will need to replenish these chips every so often during the smoking. Try a variety of flavored smoking chips. Hickory and mesquite are the most popular, but cherry, apple and maple chips offer great flavor as well. When in the South I like to use pecan wood. It provides a sweet nutty flavor to my smoked ribs.

When the coals are hot, place a dish of hot water in the bottom of the smoker. Place the grill on top of the hot coals.

It is best to marinate your ribs for 4 to 6 hours or overnight and then rub them with your favorite spice rub. Place ribs meaty side up and cover the smoker. Once an hour, check and add additional coals and smoking chips as needed, maintaining the temperature around 200 to 225°F.

Cooking Time:	Preheated 200 to 225°F smoker. Soaked smoking chips.	
	2 to 3 lb. pork spareribs and beef ribs	3 to 4 hours
	6 to 8 lb. pork picnic or pork butt roasts	5 to 6 hours
	1 to 2 lb. pork back ribs and country-style ribs	3 hours

Braising: My Favorite Cooking Method

I love cooking ribs as much as I love eating ribs.
I started out like many, boiling and steaming ribs,
but was never satisfied with the results. I then
started traveling to different BBQ competitions
in search of the best ribs. I learned to love smoked
ribs and grilled ribs but knew that the ultimate rib
had to be somewhere out there. I then met a rib
cooker by the name of Jerry Gibson. Jerry's ribs
were incredible. Nirvana was at hand. Jerry told
me that braising was the secret to great-tasting
ribs. Braising is done in your oven and is a combination of roasting and steaming.

Preheat oven to 325°F. Rub ribs with your
favorite BBQ seasoning. Place ribs meat side
down overlapping in a roasting pan. Add 1 to
2 cups of liquid (juice, beer or water) and place
3 to 4 slices of lemon on the back of each rack of
ribs. Cover and braise until fully cooked and the
bones can be pulled cleanly from the meat.

Cooking Time:	Preheated 325°F oven.	
	2 to 3 lb. pork spareribs and beef ribs, beef short ribs	2 to 3 hours
	1 to 2 lb. pork back ribs and country-style ribs	2 to 2½ hours
	1 lb. lamb ribs	1½ hours

Jalapeño Honey Garlic Baby Back Ribs

That's not a mistake in the recipe—I mean 12 cloves of garlic. You can never have enough garlic. These ribs are very sticky. On a sticky scale from 1 to 10, they rate an 11.

4 racks	pork baby back ribs (each 1¹/₂ lb.)		4	jalapeño peppers, finely chopped
2 tbsp.	Bone Dust BBQ Spice (page 99)		2 cups	honey
2	lemons, sliced		1 cup	chicken stock
¹/₂ cup	lemon juice		¹/₂ cup	rice vinegar
1 can	ginger ale		2 tbsp.	prepared mustard
			2 tsp.	dry mustard
Jalapeño Honey Garlic Sauce			2 tsp.	black mustard seeds
2 tbsp.	vegetable oil		1 tsp.	black pepper
12 cloves	garlic, minced		¹/₂ tsp.	cayenne pepper
1	small onion, finely chopped			Salt to taste

1. Preheat oven to 325°F.
2. Using a sharp knife, score the membrane on the backside of the ribs in a diamond pattern. Rub with the Bone Dust BBQ Spice, pressing the seasoning into the meat.
3. Lay the ribs meat side down in a roasting pan. Lay 3 to 4 slices of lemon on the back of each rib. Pour in the lemon juice and ginger ale. Cover tightly with lid or foil.
4. Braise ribs until tender, 2 to 2¹/₂ hours. Let cool slightly.
5. Meanwhile, prepare the sauce. Heat the oil in a medium saucepan over medium-high heat. Sauté the garlic, onion and jalapeños until tender, 2 to 3 minutes. Add honey, chicken stock, rice vinegar, prepared mustard, dry mustard and mustard seeds. Bring to a boil, reduce heat to low and simmer for 15 minutes, stirring occasionally. Season with black pepper, cayenne pepper and salt.
6. Preheat grill to medium-high.
7. Grill ribs, basting with sauce, for 6 to 8 minutes per side.
8. Cut between every third rib and serve.

Serves 4 to 6

Guinness-Braised Baby Back Ribs with Sweet Molasses BBQ Sauce

This recipe calls for 4 cans of Guinness. Two cans are for the ribs and two cans are for you to drink while preparing this recipe. Guinness rules!

4 racks	pork baby back ribs (each 1¹/₂ lb.)		4 cloves	garlic, crushed
			4 cans	Guinness Irish stout
2 tbsp.	Bone Dust BBQ Spice (page 99)		2 cups	gourmet BBQ sauce
1	large onion, sliced		¹/₂ cup	molasses

1. Preheat oven to 325°F.
2. Using a sharp knife, score the membrane on the backside of the ribs in a diamond pattern. Rub with the Bone Dust BBQ Spice, pressing the seasoning into the meat.
3. Spread the onion and garlic in a roasting pan. Lay the ribs on top meat side down. Pour in 2 cans of Guinness. Cover tightly with lid or foil.
4. Braise ribs until tender, 2 to 2¹/₂ hours. Let cool slightly. Remove ribs from pan and set aside.
5. Pour Guinness mixture into a large saucepan. Bring to a boil and reduce liquid by half. Stir in the BBQ sauce and molasses. Return to a boil, stirring, and remove from heat. Purée sauce until smooth.
6. Preheat grill to medium-high.
7. Grill ribs, basting with sauce, for 6 to 8 minutes per side.
8. Cut between every third rib and serve.

Serves 4 to 6

Chili Pineapple Baby Back Ribs

This is a sweet-with-heat glazing sauce. It is great not only on ribs but drizzled over ice cream too. Try my Smoked Chocolate Crème Fraîche Ice Cream on page 225.

4 racks	pork baby back ribs (each 1 1/2 lb.)		4 cloves	garlic, minced
6 tbsp.	Indonesian Cinnamon Rub (page 105)		1/2	small onion, finely chopped
2	onions, sliced		1 tbsp.	crushed red chilies
3 cups	pineapple juice		1	can (14 oz.) crushed pineapple
			1 cup	corn syrup
Chili Pineapple BBQ Glazing Sauce			1/2 cup	water
			1 tbsp.	prepared horseradish
2 tbsp.	vegetable oil			Salt

1. Preheat oven to 325°F.
2. Using a sharp knife, score the membrane on the backside of the ribs in a diamond pattern. Rub with the Cinnamon Rub, pressing the seasoning into the meat.
3. Spread the onions in a roasting pan. Lay the ribs on top meat side down. Pour the pineapple juice over the ribs. Cover tightly with lid or foil.
4. Braise ribs until the meat is tender, 2 to 2 1/2 hours. Let cool slightly.
5. Meanwhile, prepare the glazing sauce. Heat the oil in a medium saucepan over medium-high heat. Sauté the garlic, onion and crushed chilies until the onion is tender, 2 to 3 minutes. Stir in the pineapple and its juice, corn syrup, water and horseradish. Bring to a boil, reduce heat to low and simmer for 15 minutes, stirring occasionally. Season to taste with salt.
6. Preheat grill to medium-high.
7. Grill ribs, basting with the glazing sauce, until slightly charred, 6 to 8 minutes per side.
8. Cut between every third rib and serve.

Serves 4 to 6

Baby Back Ribs with Apricot Glazing Sauce

I am—as you can tell—a lover of ribs. They're my favorite food. When cooked till tender and glazed with a rich, flavorful sauce, nothing beats good ribs. This apricot glaze is made easy by using apricot jam. It's sweet with a little heat.

4 racks	pork baby back ribs (each 1¹/₂ lb.)		4 cloves	garlic, minced
2 tbsp.	Bone Dust BBQ Spice (page 99)		1 tbsp.	minced fresh ginger
			1 tbsp.	crushed red chilies
2	oranges, sliced		2 cups	apricot jam
2 cups	orange juice		¹/₂ cup	honey
			¹/₂ cup	water
Apricot Glazing Sauce			¹/₄ cup	cider vinegar
2 tbsp.	vegetable oil		1 tbsp.	chopped fresh sage
				Salt

1. Preheat oven to 325°F.
2. Using a sharp knife, score the membrane on the backside of the ribs in a diamond pattern. Rub with the Bone Dust BBQ Spice, pressing the seasoning into the meat.
3. Lay the ribs meat side down in a roasting pan. Lay 3 to 4 slices of orange on the back of each rib. Pour in orange juice. Cover tightly with lid or foil.
4. Braise ribs until tender, 2 to 2¹/₂ hours. Let cool slightly.
5. Meanwhile, prepare the glazing sauce. Heat the oil in a medium saucepan over medium-high heat. Sauté the garlic, ginger and crushed chilies until tender, 2 minutes. Add the apricot jam, honey, water, vinegar and sage, whisking until smooth. Bring to a boil, reduce heat to low and simmer, stirring occasionally, for 15 minutes. Season to taste with salt.
6. Preheat grill to medium-high.
7. Grill ribs, basting with glazing sauce, for 6 to 8 minutes per side.
8. Cut between every third rib and toss with remaining glazing sauce.

Serves 4 to 6

Dave's Beer Steamed Baby Back Ribs with Island Stinger BBQ Sauce

Dave Nichol is an inspiration, and I have had the pleasure of cooking for him many times. Dave is very particular about ribs. He believes that the best ribs are steamed. I have cooked hundreds of racks of ribs for Dave at many events and he always insists that we steam them. For Dave, a rib is not good until the super-tender meat easily pulls free from the bone.

4 bottles	Dave's Beer or hard lemonade		**Island Stinger BBQ Sauce**	
4 racks	pork baby back ribs (each 1¹/₂ lb.)		1 bottle	Dave's Island Stinger or hard lemonade
2 tbsp.	Bone Dust BBQ Spice (page 99)		1 cup	honey
			1 cup	gourmet BBQ sauce
			¹/₂ cup	orange marmalade
			2 tbsp.	cider vinegar
				Salt and pepper

1. Pour the beer into a steamer pot and bring to a boil. Rub the ribs with the Bone Dust BBQ Spice, pressing the seasoning into the meat.
2. Steam ribs on a steamer rack until tender, about 1¹/₂ hours.
3. Meanwhile, prepare the sauce. In a medium saucepan, whisk together the Island Stinger, honey, BBQ sauce, marmalade and vinegar. Bring to a boil, reduce heat and simmer for 15 minutes, stirring occasionally. If necessary, thicken with a little cornstarch stirred into water. Remove from heat and season to taste with salt and pepper.
4. Preheat grill to medium-high.
5. Grill ribs, basting liberally with the sauce, for 8 to 10 minutes per side.
6. Cut between every third rib and serve.

Serves 4 to 6

Cherry Whisky Smoked Baby Back Ribs

I love to smoke ribs. In fact I love to smoke just about anything. Low and slow is the key to great smoked ribs, so patience is everything. If you want to cut down the time involved, first steam the ribs until they are tender, and then smoke them for 2 hours to allow the smoke flavor to permeate the meat.

4 racks	pork baby back ribs (each 1½ lb.)
2 cups	cherry whisky
2 cups	water
½ cup	sugar
¼ cup	salt
	Cherry smoking chips
¼ cup	Bone Dust BBQ Spice (page 99)

Cherry Whisky Glazing Sauce

1	small onion, diced
4 cloves	garlic, minced
1 cup	gourmet BBQ sauce
½ cup	cherry whisky
½ cup	honey
¼ cup	grape jelly
2 tbsp.	vegetable oil
	Cayenne pepper, salt and black pepper

1. Using a sharp knife, score the membrane on the backside of the ribs in a diamond pattern. Place the ribs in a roasting pan. Combine the cherry whisky, water, sugar and salt; pour over the ribs. Marinate, covered and refrigerated, for at least 4 hours or overnight.
2. Prepare your smoker according to manufacturer's instructions to a temperature of 225°F. (See page 115.) Soak cherry chips in water while coals are heating.
3. Remove ribs from marinade (reserving marinade for basting) and rub with Bone Dust BBQ Spice, pressing the spices into the meat.
4. Place ribs in smoker and add soaked wood chips to coals. Close lid and smoke ribs, basting every hour with reserved marinade, until the ribs are tender and the bones wiggle a little when pulled, 4 to 5 hours. Maintain a constant temperature of 225°F, and replenish coals, water and wood chips as needed.

5. Meanwhile, prepare the glazing sauce. In a medium saucepan, combine the onion, garlic, BBQ sauce, cherry whisky, honey, grape jelly and oil. Bring to a boil, stirring. Reduce heat and simmer for 15 minutes. Season to taste with a pinch of cayenne pepper, salt and black pepper. Remove from heat.
6. Preheat grill to medium-high.
7. Grill ribs, basting liberally with glazing sauce, for 10 to 12 minutes per side.
8. Cut between every third rib and serve.

Serves 4 to 6

Apple Juice Boiled Spareribs with Apple Butter BBQ Sauce

The key to this recipe is lots of apple butter. The BBQ sauce is also great drizzled over baked sweet potatoes.

2 racks	pork spareribs (each 2 to 3 lb.)
8 cups	apple juice
2 tbsp.	minced fresh ginger
2 tsp.	salt
1	cinnamon stick
2	bay leaves

Apple Butter BBQ Sauce

1 tbsp.	vegetable oil
4 cloves	garlic, minced
1 cup	apple butter
1 cup	gourmet BBQ sauce
1/2 cup	brown sugar
1/2 cup	apple juice
1 tbsp.	Worcestershire sauce
1 tbsp.	chopped fresh thyme
	Salt and pepper to taste

1. Using a sharp knife, score the membrane on the backside of the ribs in a diamond pattern.
2. In a large pot, bring the apple juice, ginger, salt, cinnamon stick and bay leaves to a boil. Add the spareribs, reduce heat to medium-low, cover and simmer until ribs are tender, about 2 hours. Remove ribs from pot and let cool slightly.
3. Meanwhile, prepare the sauce. Heat the oil in a medium saucepan over medium-high heat. Sauté the garlic for 1 minute. Stir in the apple butter, BBQ sauce, brown sugar, apple juice and Worcestershire sauce. Bring to a boil, stirring. Reduce heat to medium-low and simmer for 15 minutes. Remove from heat and stir in thyme, salt and pepper.
4. Preheat grill to medium-high.
5. Season ribs with salt and pepper. Grill ribs, basting liberally with sauce, for 8 to 10 minutes per side.
6. Cut between every third rib and serve.

Serves 4

Rum and Raisin Glazed Grilled Spareribs

While in Jamaica I had a refreshing beverage of Appleton rum and ginger beer served over ice. It was the inspiration for these ribs.

2 racks	pork spareribs (each 2 to 3 lb.)		1 cup	water
1/2 cup	RED-RUM Rub (page 109)		1/2 cup	golden raisins
2 cans	ginger beer		1/2 cup	honey
1/4 cup	dark rum		1/4 cup	brown sugar
			1/4 cup	dark rum
Rum and Raisin Glazing Sauce			1 tbsp.	chopped fresh thyme
2 tbsp.	vegetable oil		2 tsp.	cornstarch, dissolved in 2 tbsp. water
1	small onion, finely chopped			Salt and cracked black pepper
1 tbsp.	finely chopped fresh ginger			

1. Using a sharp knife, score the membrane on the backside of the ribs in a diamond pattern. Rub with RED-RUM Rub, pressing the seasoning into the meat. Lay the ribs meat side down in a roasting pan and pour in the ginger beer and rum to cover. Marinate, covered and refrigerated, at least 4 hours or overnight.
2. To prepare the glazing sauce, heat the oil in a medium saucepan over medium-high heat. Sauté the onion and ginger until tender, 2 to 3 minutes. Stir in the water, raisins, honey, brown sugar, rum and thyme. Bring to a boil, reduce heat and simmer for 15 minutes, stirring occasionally. Stir in cornstarch mixture; return to a boil, stirring, until thickened. Remove from heat and season to taste with salt and pepper.
3. Preheat grill to medium.
4. Grill ribs, turning every 15 minutes, for 1 hour. Grill for another 30 minutes, basting frequently with the sauce.
5. Cut between every third rib and serve.

Serves 4

Stuffed Pork Ribs with Curried Fruit Compote

Octoberfest in Kitchener is always a good time, with plenty of cold beer and lots of good food. Just outside Kitchener is a little restaurant called the Blue Moon, where I first had delicious tender ribs stuffed with a ton of moist bread stuffing. Serve these ribs with a few pints of ice-cold beer.

2 racks	pork spareribs (each 2 to 3 lb.)		2 stalks	celery, diced
2 tbsp.	Bone Dust BBQ Spice (page 99)		6 slices	bacon, fully cooked and chopped
1	lemon, thinly sliced		1 cup	diced dried apricots
2 cups	apple juice		1/2 cup	golden raisins
			1 tbsp.	chopped fresh rosemary
Stuffing			1/2 cup	boiling water
1 loaf	enriched white bread (about 22 slices)		1/4 cup	melted butter
				Salt and pepper
2 cloves	garlic, minced			Vegetable oil
1	onion, diced			

1. Preheat oven to 325°F.
2. Using a sharp knife, score the membrane on the backside of the ribs in a diamond pattern. Rub with Bone Dust BBQ Spice, pressing the seasoning into the meat. Lay the ribs meat side down in a roasting pan. Lay 3 to 4 slices of lemon on the back of each rib; pour in apple juice. Cover tightly with lid or foil.
3. Braise ribs until tender, 2 to 2 1/2 hours. Let cool slightly. Reduce oven temperature to 200°F.
4. While ribs are cooling, prepare the stuffing. Cut the bread into 1/2-inch cubes. Spread on a baking sheet and heat in the oven until dry, about 30 minutes.
5. In a large bowl, combine the dried bread, garlic, onion, celery, bacon, apricots, raisins and rosemary. Add the boiling water and melted butter, stirring to fully mix. Season to taste with salt and pepper. The stuffing should hold together but still be moist.

6. Lay 1 pork rib, curved side up, on a work surface. Stuff the curved side of the rib with all of the bread stuffing, pressing it firmly to form a log along the inside of the rib. Place the other rib, curved side down, on top of the stuffing, pressing firmly so it adheres. Tie the ribs together with string at 2-inch intervals. Brush the ribs with a little vegetable oil.
7. Preheat grill to medium.
8. Grill ribs away from direct heat, with the lid closed, until lightly charred and the stuffing is hot, 10 to 15 minutes per side. (Using indirect heat will enable you to use your grill more like an oven and grill-roast the ribs.) Remove ribs from grill and let stand for 5 minutes.
9. Cut between every second bone and serve with Curried Fruit Compote (recipe follows).

Serves 4

Curried Fruit Compote

1 cup	diced fresh pineapple	1/4 cup	plum sauce
1/2 cup	diced dried apricots	1/4 cup	water
1/2 cup	candied cherries, halved	1 tbsp.	minced fresh ginger
1/4 cup	candied orange peel	1 tbsp.	curry paste
1/4 cup	golden raisins		Salt
1/2 cup	corn syrup		

1. In a medium saucepan, combine the pineapple, apricots, cherries, orange peel, raisins, corn syrup, plum sauce, water, ginger and curry paste. Bring to a boil, stirring. Reduce heat to medium-low and simmer for 15 minutes. Season to taste with salt. Let cool.

Makes about 3 1/2 cups

Raspberry Chipotle Glazed Spareribs

This sweet and spicy sauce is a perfect match for meaty spareribs. Chipotle chilies in adobo sauce can be found in specialty food stores and in the ethnic section of supermarkets. A chipotle chili is a smoked jalapeño pepper. If you're short on time, use Dan-T's Raspberry Chipotle Sauce instead of making the glaze.

2 racks	pork spareribs (each 2 to 3 lb.)		1/2 cup	raspberry jam
3 tbsp.	Bone Dust BBQ Spice (page 99)		1/2 cup	water
3 to 4 cups	cranberry juice		1/4 cup	chipotle chilies in adobo sauce
			1/4 cup	raspberry vinegar
Raspberry Chipotle Glaze			1 tbsp.	chopped fresh ginger
1 pint	raspberries		1 tbsp.	chopped fresh mint
1 cup	honey			Salt and pepper

1. Using a sharp knife, score the membrane on the backside of the ribs in a diamond pattern. Rub with the Bone Dust BBQ Spice, pressing the seasoning into the meat. Lay the ribs in a roasting pan and pour in enough cranberry juice to cover. Marinate, covered and refrigerated, at least 4 hours or overnight.
2. Preheat oven to 350°F.
3. Discard marinade and place ribs on a rack in the roasting pan. Roast ribs until tender, 75 to 90 minutes.
4. Meanwhile, prepare the glaze. In a small saucepan combine the raspberries, honey, jam, water, chilies, vinegar, ginger and mint. Bring to a boil, stirring. Reduce heat to low and simmer, stirring occasionally, for 15 minutes. Season to taste with salt and pepper. Purée the sauce until smooth. Let cool.
5. Preheat grill to medium-high.
6. Grill ribs, basting with lots of glaze, for 8 to 10 minutes per side.
7. Cut between every third rib and serve.

Serves 4

Asian-Spiced Country-Style Pork Ribs

Marinating country-style ribs helps tenderize them and boosts their flavor. Patience is everything with this recipe—low and slow, with a few beer chasers.
Sambal oelek is a Thai garlic chili sauce, available in Asian markets.

2 racks	country-style pork ribs (each 1 to 1¹/₂ lb.)	1 cup	water
¹/₄ cup	Bone Dust BBQ Spice (page 99)	¹/₂ cup	light corn syrup
		¹/₄ cup	lime juice
4 cloves	garlic, minced	¹/₄ cup	rice wine vinegar
1 cup	ketchup	1 tbsp.	chopped fresh cilantro
		1 tbsp.	sambal oelek

1. Rub the ribs with the Bone Dust BBQ Spice, pressing the seasoning into the meat. Place in a roasting pan.
2. Stir together the garlic, ketchup, water, corn syrup, lime juice, vinegar, cilantro and sambal oelek. Pour over the ribs, turning to coat. Marinate, covered and refrigerated, for 6 to 8 hours.
3. Preheat grill to medium-high.
4. Remove ribs from marinade (reserving marinade for basting) and grill ribs, turning frequently and basting with reserved marinade, until the ribs are cooked and tender and a meat thermometer reads 160°F, 40 to 50 minutes.
5. Cut into 1-inch-thick slices and serve.

Serves 6 to 8

Grilled Spicy Thai Chili Back Rib Tail Pieces

Hot and spicy to start, and sticky to finish. These are great rib ticklers for the start to a great barbecue.

2 lb.	pork back rib tail pieces
2 tbsp.	Bone Dust BBQ Spice (page 99)
1/2 cup	coconut milk
1/2 cup	water
1/4 cup	lime juice

Spicy Thai Chili Glaze

3	green onions, finely chopped
3/4 cup	plum sauce
1/2 cup	sweet Thai chili sauce
1/4 cup	brown sugar
1/4 cup	soy sauce
1/4 cup	dry sherry
2 tbsp.	lime juice
2 tbsp.	rice wine vinegar
1 tbsp.	chopped fresh cilantro

1. Rub the rib pieces with the Bone Dust BBQ Spice, pressing the seasoning into the meat. In a glass dish large enough to hold the rib pieces in one layer, whisk together the coconut milk, water and lime juice. Add the rib pieces, turning to coat. Marinate, covered and refrigerated, for at least 6 hours or overnight.
2. To prepare the glaze, in a bowl whisk together the green onions, plum sauce, chili sauce, brown sugar, soy sauce, sherry, lime juice, vinegar and cilantro.
3. Preheat grill to medium-high.
4. Grill rib pieces, basting generously with the glaze, for 5 to 6 minutes per side.
5. Serve immediately.

Serves 2 to 4

The Boneless Rib with Mango BBQ Sauce

Sometimes you just want to eat meat and forget about all the bones. This recipe uses the pork loin and produces a tender, succulent boneless rib. Slow braising allows for maximum tenderness and maximum flavor. This one's all meat, baby. No bones about it.

1	boneless pork loin (3 to 4 lb. and about 1 foot long)	1	jalapeño pepper, seeded and finely chopped
1/2 cup	RED-RUM Rub (page 109)	1 1/2 cups	gourmet BBQ sauce
2	lemons, thinly sliced	1/2 cup	ketchup
2 bottles	Dave's Island Stinger or hard lemonade	1/2 cup	honey
		1/4 cup	orange juice
Mango BBQ Sauce		1 tbsp.	minced fresh ginger
		1 tbsp.	lemon juice
1	large ripe mango, peeled and finely chopped		Salt to taste

1. Cut the pork loin lengthwise into 3 equal pieces. The pieces should look similar to a back rib but without the bones. Rub the "boneless pork rib" with the RED-RUM Rub, pressing the seasoning into the meat. Place pork in a roasting pan. Lay 3 to 4 lemon slices on each "rib." Pour the Island Stingers over the meat. Cover tightly with lid or foil and marinate, refrigerated, for 2 to 4 hours.
2. Preheat oven to 375°F.
3. Braise ribs for 1 1/2 hours. Let cool slightly.
4. Meanwhile, prepare the Mango BBQ Sauce. In a medium bowl, whisk together the mango, jalapeño, BBQ sauce, ketchup, honey, orange juice, ginger, lemon juice and salt.
5. Preheat grill to medium-high.
6. Grill "ribs," basting liberally with the sauce, until lightly charred and hot, 3 to 4 minutes per side.
7. Cut pork into 1-inch-thick slices to resemble ribs. Transfer to a serving platter and serve immediately with remaining sauce for dipping.

Serves 8 to 10

Spicy Korean Beef Short Ribs

My version of these tasty ribs—known as bulkogi—*is easy to prepare. This is a perfect recipe to start any backyard barbecue.*

4	green onions, finely chopped	2 tbsp.	sambal oelek (Thai garlic chili sauce)
6 cloves	garlic, minced	1 tbsp.	chopped fresh cilantro
1/4 cup	brown sugar	1 tbsp.	sesame oil
1/4 cup	vegetable oil	2 tsp.	toasted sesame seeds
1/4 cup	soy sauce	2 tsp.	cracked black pepper
1/4 cup	rice vinegar	4 lb.	beef short ribs, cut across the bones 1/2 inch thick (about 15 to 20 pieces)
1/4 cup	dry sherry		
2 tbsp.	chopped fresh ginger		

1. In a glass dish large enough to hold the ribs in one layer, whisk together the green onions, garlic, brown sugar, vegetable oil, soy sauce, rice vinegar, sherry, ginger, sambal oelek, cilantro, sesame oil, sesame seeds and pepper. Add the ribs, turning to coat. Marinate, covered and refrigerated, at least 4 hours or overnight.
2. Preheat grill to medium-high.
3. Remove ribs from marinade. Pour marinade into a small saucepan. Bring to a boil, reduce heat and simmer for 5 minutes. Remove from heat.
4. Grill ribs, basting liberally with heated marinade, 2 to 3 minutes per side.

Serves 4 to 6

Big Bones Beef Ribs with Jack's Devilishly Good BBQ Sauce

Two-fisted eating is a requirement when tackling the monster beef rib. You know you have done a good job of eating when your hands, arms, chest and face are covered with sticky sauce.

Ask your butcher to cut the racks in half lengthwise across the bones to give you a narrow rack of ribs, similar to pork spareribs.

2 racks	prime rib of beef back ribs (each 5 lb.)	2 cups	hickory smoke–flavored BBQ sauce
1/4 cup	Great Canadian Steak Spice (page 98)	1 cup	steak sauce
		1/2 cup	maple syrup
		1/4 cup	Jack Daniel's Sour Mash Whiskey
Jack's Devilishly Good BBQ Sauce		2 tbsp.	malt vinegar
2 tbsp.	vegetable oil	1 tbsp.	chopped fresh thyme
1	small onion, diced	1 tbsp.	cracked black pepper
4 cloves	garlic, chopped		Salt to taste

1. Rub the racks with the Steak Spice, pressing the seasoning into the meat. Marinate, covered at room temperature, for 30 minutes.
2. To prepare the sauce, heat the oil in a medium saucepan over medium-high heat. Sauté the onion and garlic until tender. Stir in the BBQ sauce, steak sauce, maple syrup, Jack Daniel's, vinegar, thyme, pepper and salt. Bring to a boil, reduce heat to low and simmer for 15 minutes, stirring occasionally.
3. Preheat grill to medium-high.
4. Grill ribs until seared, 4 to 5 minutes per side. Move ribs to the upper rack of the grill, close the lid and grill-roast ribs, basting occasionally with the sauce, until tender, 30 to 45 minutes.
5. Remove ribs from grill and glaze with extra sauce. Serve immediately with lots of wet naps and napkins.

Serves 6 to 8

Five Doors North Buffalo Ribs with Amaretto BBQ Sauce

Buffalo ribs are not the easiest thing to find, so you may have to order them from your butcher. They are similar to beef ribs but they have a stronger, gamier flavor. Make sure you cook them until they're very tender. They're a bit expensive, and you do not want to spend good money only to have tough, undercooked ribs.

Five Doors North is a Toronto restaurant owned by Chef Vito Rizzuto. He prepared these for me one night but would not divulge his recipe. This is what I came up with.

2 racks	buffalo ribs (each 3 to 4 lb.)
1/4 cup	Bone Dust BBQ Spice (page 99)
2 bottles	beer

Amaretto BBQ Sauce

2 cups	hickory smoke–flavored BBQ sauce
1/2 cup	brown sugar
1/4 cup	steak sauce
1/4 cup	ketchup
1/4 cup	amaretto
	Salt and pepper

1. Rub the ribs with the Bone Dust BBQ Spice, pressing the seasoning into the meat. Place ribs in a roasting pan and marinate at room temperature for 30 minutes.
2. Preheat oven to 375°F.
3. Pour the beer over the ribs. Cover tightly with lid or foil.
4. Braise ribs until very tender, about 1 1/2 hours. Let cool slightly.
5. Meanwhile, prepare the sauce by whisking together the BBQ sauce, brown sugar, steak sauce, ketchup and amaretto. Season to taste with salt and pepper.
6. Preheat grill to medium-high.
7. Grill ribs, basting liberally with the sauce, for 8 to 10 minutes per side.
8. Slice between every bone and serve immediately.

Serves 8

Honey Mustard Grilled Lamb Ribs

Lamb ribs are a Greek party favorite, and they're one of my favorite foods. If you've never had them, make a point of getting some and munching away. You may have to order these from your butcher.

8 racks	lamb ribs
1/4 cup	Herb Mustard Rub (page 104)
1	large onion, sliced
12 cloves	garlic, minced
2	lemons, thinly sliced
1 tbsp.	chopped fresh rosemary
1 to 2 cups	white wine

Honey Mustard Glazing Sauce

2	green onions, finely chopped
1 cup	honey
1/2 cup	prepared mustard
2 tbsp.	old-fashioned grainy mustard
2 tbsp.	lemon juice
1 tbsp.	chopped fresh parsley
	Salt and pepper to taste

1. Preheat oven to 325°F.
2. Using a sharp knife, score the ribs on both sides in a diamond pattern. Rub with the Herb Mustard Rub, pressing the seasoning into the meat.
3. Place the onion, garlic, lemon slices, rosemary and wine in a roasting pan. Arrange ribs on top. Cover tightly with lid or foil.
4. Braise ribs until tender, about 1 1/2 hours. Let cool slightly.
5. To prepare the glazing sauce, whisk together the green onions, honey, prepared mustard, grainy mustard, lemon juice, parsley, salt and pepper.
6. Preheat grill to medium-high.
7. Grill ribs, basting with the glazing sauce, for 4 to 5 minutes per side.
8. Cut between every second bone and serve with grilled potatoes.

Serves 4

Lip-Smacking Tenderloins

Steak Basics

Beef

Steak Cuts

Tenderloin

Of all the steak cuts, the tenderloin is the most tender. The tenderloin comes from the short loin of beef; it lies between the rib and the sirloin and never really does anything but lie there and be tender. The tenderloin may be cooked whole or cut into wonderfully tender steaks. Be careful not to overcook this cut. It does not have a lot of fat, so it tends to dry out and become tough the more it cooks.

Striploin

The striploin steak is one of the most popular cuts of beef. It comes from the top loin muscle in the short loin of beef. It is best grilled to medium-rare and is often served with a peppercorn sauce. This steak is known by many names, the most popular being the New York strip steak and Kansas City steak. A bone-in striploin steak is known as a shell steak.

Rib-Eye Steak

This steak is cut from between the rib and chuck section. The bone-in rib steak is also known as the cowboy steak. The rib steak is an extremely tender cut of beef. This steak is heavily marbled with fat, giving it maximum flavor. It is best to grill this steak to medium-rare, which allows the internal fat to melt and bring out the natural juices and flavor.

T-Bone Steak

This steak is named after the shape of its bone, a large T that separates the striploin from the small tenderloin. Cut from the center of the short loin, this is a large steak, often best shared, but if you're truly hungry it is a real meal for one. I like to serve this steak with lots of sautéed onions and mushrooms and topped with crumbled blue cheese.

Porterhouse Steak

A porterhouse steak is cut from the large end of the short loin and also has the same T-shaped bone as the T-bone. It has a larger tenderloin portion and is truly a meal for two—it's sometimes called the king of steaks. It is often cut into 2-inch-thick portions weighing approximately 36 oz. Rub this steak with garlic, black pepper and fresh rosemary and grill it over medium-high heat.

Sirloin Steak

Cut from the area between the short loin and round, the sirloin has three main muscles. Cut into steaks, they are quite flavorful but require marinating to make them a little more tender. A teriyaki marinade is the most popular marinade used on sirloin steaks.

Flank Steak

The flank steak comes from the lower hind region of beef. It is a tougher cut of steak that requires marinating to make it tender. As it does not have a lot of internal fat, be careful not to overcook it. Marinated in an Asian marinade, this steak will have great flavor. It is best sliced thinly when served and is a great steak for a salad or steak sandwich.

Hanger Steak

The hanger steak hangs between the rib cage and loin cage. Hanger steaks have a little stronger flavor than regular steaks and need to be very fresh. Ask your butcher for this tender cut of beef, which isn't usually found in grocery stores. Marinate it with stronger-flavored herbs and spices and lots of garlic. It is best cooked rare to medium and sliced thinly.

Cooking Steak

How Do You Like Your Steak Cooked?

Blue Rare: A blue rare steak is quickly charred on the outside and barely cooked on the inside. For best results, bring the steak to room temperature before cooking.

Rare: A rare steak has a cool red center.

Medium-Rare: A medium-rare steak has a warm red center.

Medium: A medium steak has a pink center and the juices are clear.

Medium-Well: A medium-well steak has a hot pink center and the juices are clear.

Well-Done: A well-done steak is gray throughout without any trace of pink and the juices are clear.

Super Well Done: This steak is weighted with a brick until heavily charred on the outside and without any trace of pink and no juices inside.

How to Test for Doneness for Your Perfect Steak

The best way to test for doneness on a steak is to use a meat thermometer.

Blue rare	130°F
Rare	130 to 140°F
Medium-rare	140 to 145°F
Medium	145 to 150°F
Medium-well	150 to 160°F
Well-done	160 to 170°F
Super well done	170°F plus

The next best method to test for doneness is the Hand Touch Method. Shake one hand loose so that it is completely relaxed. With your other hand, touch the soft fleshy part of your relaxed hand at the base of your thumb. This soft texture is similar to the texture of a blue rare to rare steak.

Now touch your thumb and forefinger together and again touch the base of your thumb. This texture is similar to a medium-rare steak.

Next, touch your thumb to your middle finger. This firmer texture is similar to the texture of a medium steak.

Next, touch your thumb to your fourth finger. The semi-firm texture at the base of your thumb is similar to a medium-well steak.

Lastly, touch your thumb to your pinky finger. The very firm texture at the base of your thumb is similar to a well-done steak.

This method of testing for a steak is relatively easy and you will never find yourself looking for a thermometer while grilling.

One last note: never cut the meat to test for doneness. Cutting the steak lets all the natural juices escape, leaving you with a dry and tasteless piece of meat.

Bacon-Wrapped Fillet with Lobster and Cheddar Topping

I love surf and turf, especially when the surf is lobster. You can use thawed frozen lobster or crab meat, but be sure to squeeze out the excess moisture first.

6 to 12 slices	thick-cut bacon		1 cup	cream cheese, softened
6	beef tenderloin fillets (each about 8 oz.)		1	egg white
2 tbsp.	Great Canadian Steak Spice (page 98)		1/4 cup	fresh bread crumbs
			1 tbsp.	chopped fresh parsley
			1 tbsp.	lemon juice
Lobster and Cheddar Topping			Pinch	cayenne pepper
1 1/2 cups	cooked lobster meat			Salt and pepper to taste
1 1/2 cups	shredded aged white Cheddar cheese			

1. Fry the bacon until slightly cooked and still flexible, 2 to 3 minutes per side. Drain on paper towels.
2. Rub the fillets all over with the Steak Spice, pressing the seasoning into the meat. Wrap each fillet with a slice of bacon. (Use a half slice extra if the bacon does not quite make it all the way around.) Seal with a toothpick and set aside to marinate for 30 minutes.
3. Meanwhile, prepare the topping. In a bowl combine the lobster meat, Cheddar cheese, cream cheese, egg white, bread crumbs, parsley, lemon juice, cayenne pepper, salt and pepper.
4. Preheat grill to medium-high.
5. Grill fillets for 4 to 5 minutes per side for medium-rare and until the bacon is crispy. During the last 2 minutes of cooking, evenly spread 2 tbsp. of the topping on each steak. Close the lid until the topping is heated through.
6. Remove fillets from grill. Remove toothpicks, and serve with extra topping.

Serves 6

Grilled Beef Tenderloin with Smoked Chocolate Cream Sauce

The combination of smoke and sweet is a perfect match for grilled beef tenderloin. When I smoke white chocolate I like to use a flavored hardwood, such as cherry, apple, pecan or almond.

4	beef tenderloin fillets (each 6 oz. and 1½ inches thick)	1	shallot, finely chopped
¼ cup	Great Canadian Steak Spice (page 98)	1	small jalapeño pepper, seeded and finely chopped
		1 cup	heavy cream
Smoked Chocolate Cream Sauce		1 cup	smoked chocolate (page 222), coarsely chopped
2 tbsp.	butter	½ cup	chocolate liqueur
2 cloves	garlic, minced	1 tsp.	chopped fresh thyme
			Salt and pepper to taste

1. Preheat grill to medium-high.
2. Rub the fillets all over with the Steak Spice, pressing the seasoning into the meat. Set aside.
3. To prepare the sauce, melt the butter in a small saucepan over medium-high heat. Sauté the garlic, shallot and jalapeño until tender, 1 to 2 minutes. Stir in ¼ cup of the cream; bring to a boil. Reduce heat to low. Stirring constantly, add the smoked chocolate a little at a time, alternating with the remaining cream.
4. Gently simmer until thickened, about 5 minutes. Whisk in the chocolate liqueur, thyme, salt and pepper. Remove from heat and keep warm.
5. Grill fillets for 4 to 5 minutes per side for medium-rare.
6. Remove fillets from grill and thinly slice across the grain. Serve drizzled with the sauce.

Serves 4

Rum-Soaked Jerk Strip Steak with Jerk Butter

I cooked these babies while filming my television show King of the Q. *There we were on the beach grilling thick steaks that were spicy hot and full of flavor. I cooked USDA Prime Aged steaks that were heavily marbled and oh so tender.*

4	New York striploin steaks (each 8 to 10 oz. and 1 inch thick)	1/2 cup	dark rum
		1/2 cup	butter, softened
1/4 cup + 2 tbsp.	Jamaican Jerk Paste (page 106)		

1. Season steaks with 2 tbsp. of the Jerk Paste, pressing the seasoning into the meat. Place steaks in a glass dish large enough to hold them in one layer. Pour over the rum, turning steaks to coat. Marinate, covered and refrigerated, for 4 hours.
2. Preheat grill to medium-high.
3. In a bowl, stir together the butter and remaining 1/4 cup of Jerk Paste.
4. Grill steaks, basting with a little jerk butter, for 4 to 5 minutes per side for medium-rare.
5. Serve immediately with an extra dollop of jerk butter.

Serves 4

Smoked New York Strip Steak

Low and slow makes these steaks sing with smoke and flavor.

6	New York striploin steaks (each 16 oz. and 2 inches thick)	
1/4 cup	Bone Dust BBQ Spice (page 99)	
	Hickory smoking chunks	

Smoked Steak Glazing Sauce

3 cloves	garlic, minced
1/2 cup	hickory smoke–flavored BBQ sauce
1/4 cup	Glayva Scotch liqueur
1/4 cup	ketchup
2 tbsp.	brown sugar
2 tbsp.	malt vinegar
1 tbsp.	chopped fresh rosemary
	Salt and pepper to taste

1. Rub the steaks with the Bone Dust BBQ Spice, pressing the seasoning into the meat. Set aside.
2. Prepare the glazing sauce. In a medium saucepan, whisk together the garlic, BBQ sauce, Glayva, ketchup, brown sugar, vinegar, rosemary, salt and pepper. Set aside.
3. Prepare your smoker according to manufacturer's instructions to a temperature of 225°F. (See page 115.) Add soaked hickory smoking chunks.
4. Place steaks on smoking rack and close the lid. Smoke steaks for 2 1/2 to 3 hours for medium-rare, replenishing smoking chips, coals and water as required.
5. About 15 minutes before steaks are done, heat glazing sauce over medium heat, stirring occasionally, until hot, 10 to 15 minutes.
6. Serve steaks immediately topped with glazing sauce.

Serves 6

Cabernet-Marinated New York Strip Steak with Caesar Compound Butter

I like my Caesar dressing loaded with garlic, anchovies and Parmesan cheese. Here I turn the ingredients of a Caesar dressing into a compound butter. A slice of steak lathered with Caesar butter is delicious.

4	New York striploin steaks (each 12 oz.)	2 tbsp.	lemon juice
		1 tbsp.	capers, coarsely chopped
2 cups	cabernet	2 tsp.	chopped fresh parsley
2 to 3 tbsp.	Great Canadian Steak Spice (page 98)	1 tsp.	cracked black pepper
		4	anchovy fillets, coarsely chopped
Caesar Compound Butter		4 cloves	garlic, minced
1/2 lb.	butter, softened		Salt to taste
1/2 cup	grated Parmesan cheese		

1. Place steaks in a glass dish large enough to hold them in one layer. Pour in the cabernet, turning to coat. Marinate, covered and refrigerated, for 2 hours.
2. Prepare the Caesar Compound Butter. In a bowl, combine the butter, Parmesan cheese, lemon juice, capers, parsley, black pepper, anchovies, garlic and salt.
3. Preheat grill to medium-high.
4. Remove the steaks from the marinade and season with the Steak Spice, pressing the seasoning into the meat. Grill steaks for 4 to 5 minutes per side for medium.
5. Thinly slice the steaks across the grain and serve topped with a dollop or two of Caesar Compound Butter.

Serves 4

Italian Diablo Rib Steak

I like to use the long and curly Italian green hot chilies. Their heat is sweet and is accentuated by grilling or roasting.

4	boneless rib steaks (each 12 oz. and 1¹/₂ inches thick)	4 cloves	garlic, minced
1/4 cup	Gilroy Roasted Garlic Paste (page 97)	1	small onion, finely chopped
1/4 cup	balsamic vinegar	1 lb.	ripe plum tomatoes, seeded and coarsely chopped (or one 19-oz. can whole plum tomatoes, drained and chopped)
1/4 cup	olive oil		
1 tbsp.	cracked black pepper		
	Grated Parmesan cheese	3 tbsp.	tomato paste
		1/2 cup	chicken stock
Diablo Tomato Sauce		1	bay leaf
		1 tsp.	salt
3	Italian green hot chilies or jalapeño peppers	1 tbsp.	chopped fresh oregano or basil
1	large red bell pepper		Pepper
2 tbsp.	olive oil		

1. Rub steaks with the Gilroy Paste, pressing the seasoning into the meat. In a glass dish large enough to hold the steaks in one layer, whisk together the vinegar, oil and black pepper. Add the steaks, turning to coat. Marinate, covered and refrigerated, for 4 hours.
2. Preheat grill to medium-high.
3. To prepare the sauce, grill-roast the hot chilies and red pepper, with the lid closed, until charred and tender. Place in a bowl and cover with plastic wrap. Let stand 5 minutes. Peel, seed and chop the chilies and red pepper.
4. In a medium saucepan, heat the oil over medium heat. Cook the garlic and onion, stirring, until tender, 3 to 4 minutes. Stir in the grilled chilies and red pepper, the tomatoes, tomato paste, stock, bay leaf and salt. Bring to a low boil, reduce heat and simmer, stirring occasionally, for 30 to 40 minutes. The sauce should be thick

and a little spicy. Discard bay leaf. Stir in oregano and season to taste with salt and pepper. Remove from heat and keep warm.

5. Preheat grill to medium-high.

6. Grill steaks for 4 to 5 minutes per side for medium-rare.

7. Thinly slice steaks across the grain and serve topped with sauce and grated Parmesan cheese.

Serves 4

Thai Sirloin Steak Wraps

This is a fun recipe for the whole family to prepare. Lay out all the ingredients and let everyone make their own wrap.

6	sirloin steaks (each 6 oz.)	**Marinade**	
2 tbsp.	Indonesian Cinnamon Rub (page 105)	4	green onions, finely chopped
1	small red onion, thinly sliced	1/2 cup	hoisin sauce
1	carrot, cut into julienne strips	1/2 cup	soy sauce
1	red bell pepper, thinly sliced	1/4 cup	vegetable oil
2	green onions, thinly sliced	1/4 cup	honey
2 cups	bean sprouts	1/4 cup	rice vinegar
1 cup	Thai basil leaves	2 tbsp.	sambal oelek (Thai garlic chili sauce)
	Salt	1 tbsp.	cracked black pepper
12	green lettuce leaves	1 tbsp.	sesame oil
12	round Thai rice paper wrappers	2 tsp.	toasted sesame seeds

1. Rub the steaks with the Cinnamon Rub, pressing the seasoning into the meat.
2. Prepare the marinade. In a bowl, whisk together the chopped green onion, hoisin sauce, soy sauce, vegetable oil, honey, rice vinegar, sambal oelek, black pepper, sesame oil and sesame seeds. Set aside one-quarter of the marinade.
3. Pour remaining marinade over the steaks, turning to coat, and marinate, covered and refrigerated, for 2 to 4 hours.
4. Preheat grill to medium-high.
5. In a bowl, combine the red onion, carrot, red pepper, sliced green onions, bean sprouts and basil leaves. Add reserved marinade and toss well. Season to taste with salt.
6. Remove steaks from marinade (reserving marinade). Grill steaks for 2 to 3 minutes per side for medium-rare. Remove steaks from grill and let rest for 5 minutes. Thinly slice each steak across the grain.

7. Working with 1 rice paper wrapper at a time, soak wrapper in a bowl of warm water until flexible, about 1 minute; drain and pat dry on a tea towel. Place a lettuce leaf on the wrapper, trimming to fit if necessary. Place half a sliced steak down the center of the leaf. Top with 1/2 cup of the vegetable mixture and roll up wrap into a cone shape. Repeat to make 5 more wraps.

Serves 6

Hot and Spicy Beef Sirloin Kebabs

This is a spicy dish. The Sriacha chili sauce is the key to making this recipe zing. You can find Sriacha in Asian food stores. It's usually sold in a squeeze bottle.

4 lb.	beef sirloin	1/4 cup	Sriacha chili sauce
4 cloves	garlic, chopped	1/4 cup	rice wine vinegar
1 cup	ketchup	2 tbsp.	chopped fresh cilantro
1/2 cup	honey		Salt and pepper

1. Cut beef into 2-inch cubes.
2. In a bowl, whisk together the garlic, ketchup, honey, chili sauce, rice vinegar and cilantro. Season to taste with salt and pepper. Set aside half of the marinade.
3. Add beef to the marinade, turning to coat, and marinate, covered and refrigerated, for 4 to 6 hours.
4. Meanwhile, soak eight 10- to 12-inch bamboo skewers in hot water for 30 minutes (or use metal skewers).
5. Preheat grill to medium-high.
6. Skewer 5 or 6 pieces of beef onto each skewer. Grill skewers, basting frequently with reserved marinade, for 4 to 5 minutes per side for medium.
7. Serve with grilled vegetable kebabs.

Serves 8

The Big Man's 2002 Porterhouse Steak with Dijon Cream Sauce

I dedicate this steak to me. I am still the big man and this is my steak for 2002. Have lots of crusty bread on hand to sop up the Dijon Cream Sauce (which is also awesome with steamed fresh mussels).

4	Porterhouse steaks (each 36 oz.)	1 tbsp.	chopped fresh thyme or rosemary
1/2 cup	Malabar Pepper Rub (page 96)	2 tsp.	mustard seeds
	Olive oil	1/2 cup	dry white wine
		1 1/2 cups	heavy cream
Dijon Cream Sauce		1/4 cup	Dijon mustard
2 tbsp.	butter	1 log (125 g.)	creamy goat cheese
2	shallots, finely chopped		Salt and freshly ground black pepper
4 cloves	garlic, minced		

1. Rub each steak with the Pepper Rub, pressing the seasoning into the meat. Brush each steak with olive oil and place in a glass dish. Marinate, covered and refrigerated, for 2 to 4 hours.
2. Preheat grill to medium-high.
3. Grill steaks for 12 to 15 minutes per side for medium. Remove steaks from grill and let rest for 5 minutes.
4. While the steaks are grilling, prepare the sauce. Melt the butter in a medium saucepan over medium heat. Sauté the shallots and garlic until tender, about 2 minutes. Stir in the thyme and mustard seeds; sauté for 1 minute. Add the wine. Bring to a boil and reduce liquid by half. Add the cream, mustard and goat cheese, whisking until the cheese is incorporated. Bring to a boil, reduce heat to low and simmer until the sauce thickens, 5 to 10 minutes. If the sauce gets too thick, add a little wine to thin it down. Season to taste with salt and pepper.
5. Serve the steaks drizzled with the sauce.

Serves 4 to 8

Grilled T-Bone Steak with Stilton and Port Sauce

Three of my favorite things on one plate: a thick T-bone where the tenderloin melts in your mouth and the striploin has a thick fatty cap; Stilton; and a rich port sauce. Adjust the amount of Stilton to suit your taste—though I like lots.

4	T-bone steaks (each 20 oz. and 1½ inches thick)	1 tsp.	chopped fresh thyme
¼ cup	Great Canadian Steak Spice (page 98)	1	bay leaf
		2 cups	port
4 tbsp.	cold butter	1 cup	beef or veal stock
2	shallots, finely chopped		Salt and pepper
2 cloves	garlic, minced	1 to 2 cups	crumbled Stilton cheese

1. Rub the steaks with the Steak Spice, pressing the seasoning into the meat. Cover and marinate at room temperature for 2 hours.
2. To prepare the sauce, melt 1 tbsp. of the butter in a medium saucepan over medium-high heat. Sauté the shallots and garlic for 1 minute or until tender and transparent. Stir in the thyme, bay leaf and port. Bring to a boil and reduce liquid by half. Strain port and discard solids.
3. Return port to the saucepan and return to a boil. Stir in the stock. Reduce heat to low and simmer until the sauce has thickened, 10 to 15 minutes. Remove from heat and season to taste with salt and pepper. Whisk in the remaining 3 tbsp. of butter, 1 tbsp. at a time, until fully incorporated. Keep sauce warm.
4. Preheat grill to medium-high.
5. Grill steaks for 6 to 8 minutes per side for medium-rare, basting with melted butter during the final few minutes of grilling. Remove from grill and let steaks rest for 5 minutes.
6. Serve steaks topped with crumbled Stilton and drizzled with the sauce.

Serves 4

Grilled Flank Steak Pinwheels

This fun recipe requires a little bit of work, but the result is well worth it. As a bonus, it uses an inexpensive cut of meat.

1	flank steak (2 to 3 lb.)	2 tsp.	Worcestershire sauce
6 cloves	garlic, minced	1 tsp.	ground cumin
1/4 cup	balsamic vinegar	1 tsp.	chili powder
1/4 cup	vegetable oil, plus extra for brushing	1 tsp.	garlic powder
		2 tbsp.	vegetable oil
2 tbsp.	chopped fresh herbs	4 cloves	garlic, minced
2 tbsp.	cracked black pepper	1	small onion, diced
		2 cups	sliced assorted mushrooms
Stuffing		1/2 cup	sliced green olives
1 lb.	lean ground beef	1 tbsp.	chopped fresh thyme
1 tbsp.	Dijon mustard		Salt and pepper to taste

1. With a sharp knife, cut down the center of the flank steak, making a deep incision almost but not quite all the way through. Open up the steak so it lies flat and place between 2 sheets of plastic wrap. Lightly pound the flank steak with the smooth side of a meat mallet until 1/2 inch thick and about 12 × 18 inches.

2. In a glass dish large enough to hold the steak, whisk together the garlic, vinegar, oil, herbs and pepper. Marinate, covered and refrigerated, for 4 to 6 hours.

3. Meanwhile, prepare the stuffing. In a large bowl, combine the ground beef, mustard, Worcestershire sauce, cumin, chili powder and garlic powder.

4. Heat the vegetable oil in a large frying pan over medium-high heat. Sauté the garlic, onion and mushrooms until just tender. Let cool slightly. Add to ground meat mixture along with the olives, thyme, salt and pepper. Stir well.

5. Remove flank steak from marinade (reserving marinade). Spread the stuffing evenly over the steak, pressing it firmly onto the meat. Starting at the wide end, roll the steak into a log. Tie with string at 2-inch intervals. Cover and refrigerate for 30 minutes.

6. Meanwhile, preheat grill to medium-high.
7. Cut the flank roll into $1^1/_2$-inch pinwheel slices. Brush each pinwheel with oil and season with salt and pepper. Grill pinwheels for 4 to 5 minutes per side, basting with reserved marinade.
8. Serve immediately.

Serves 6

Grilled Shell Steak with Country Cream Gravy and Virginia Ham

Back in 1993, Pamela and I were camping in Cape Hatteras, North Carolina. We had a great day, playing in the surf and having not a care in the world—except what we should eat that evening. We were tired of watching our neighbors dine on bologna and we were out of beer. So we made a trek up the coast to buy more beer and look for a place to eat. I can't remember the name of the joint we ate at, but the grilled shell steak was awesome. Here's my version.

4	New York shell steaks, bone-in or boneless (each 16 oz.)	**Country Cream Gravy**	
1/4 cup	Malabar Pepper Rub (page 96)	2 tbsp.	butter
		2 tbsp.	all-purpose flour
1/4 cup	melted butter	2 cups	milk
8 thin slices	cured Virginia ham (each 2 oz.)	1/2 cup	heavy cream
		1 tbsp.	chopped fresh sage
		2 tsp.	Worcestershire sauce
		Pinch	cayenne pepper
			Salt and freshly ground black pepper to taste

1. Rub the steaks with the Pepper Rub, pressing the seasoning into the meat. Set aside.
2. Prepare the gravy by melting the butter over medium heat in a medium saucepan. Stir in the flour and cook, stirring, for about 1 minute, being careful not to burn it. Whisking constantly, add the milk a little at a time until smooth. Bring to boil, stirring. Reduce heat to low and simmer, stirring occasionally, for 15 minutes. Stir in the cream and cook until gravy is thick, 5 to 10 more minutes. Stir in the sage, Worcestershire sauce, cayenne, salt and black pepper. Remove from heat and keep warm.
3. Preheat grill to medium-high.
4. Grill steaks, brushing with the melted butter, for 8 to 10 minutes per side for medium.
5. Top each steak with 2 slices of Virginia ham and ladle the gravy over each steak.

Serves 4

Cedar-Planked Garlic Beef Tenderloin Roast with Smoked Garlic and Sun-dried Tomato Cream Sauce

GQ Magazine *called me a crazy Canuck. It's true!*
Use roasted garlic if you don't have a smoker.

1	beef tenderloin (4 lb.)		1/2 cup	chopped oil-packed sun-dried tomatoes
1 cup	Gilroy Roasted Garlic Paste (page 97)		1/2 cup	white wine
1/4 cup	pink peppercorns, cracked		2 cups	heavy cream
			1/2 cup	grated Parmesan cheese
			2	green onions, thinly sliced
Smoked Garlic and Sun-dried Tomato Cream Sauce				Salt and pepper
2 tbsp.	butter		Special equipment:	2 untreated cedar planks (at least 10 x 8 x 5/8 inch), soaked in water overnight
2	shallots, finely chopped			
12 cloves	smoked garlic (page 96)			

1. Rub the tenderloin with the Gilroy Paste, pressing the seasoning into the meat. Press the peppercorns evenly over the meat. Transfer to a glass dish and marinate, covered and refrigerated, for 4 to 6 hours.
2. Preheat grill to high.
3. Place soaked planks on the grill, one on top of the other, and close the lid. Let the planks heat for 2 to 3 minutes or until they start to crackle and smoke.
4. Carefully open the lid and place the tenderloin on the planks. Close the lid and roast the tenderloin for 10 minutes. Reduce heat to medium and roast for 30 to 40 minutes for medium-rare. A meat thermometer should read 135°F. Carefully open the lid (avoiding the billowing smoke) and remove beef from the grill; let rest for 10 minutes.

5. While the meat is roasting, prepare the sauce. Melt the butter in a medium saucepan over medium heat. Sauté the shallots and smoked garlic until tender, about 1 minute. Stir in the tomatoes and wine. Bring to a boil and reduce wine by one-quarter. Stir in cream and Parmesan. Return sauce to a boil, reduce heat to low and simmer until the sauce is thick, about 10 minutes. Remove from heat and stir in green onions, salt and pepper.
6. Cut the tenderloin into 1-inch-thick slices and serve with the sauce.

Serves 8

Grilled Veal Chops with Mushroom Fricassee and Buffalo Mozzarella

I prepared this dish for CART race-car driver Roberto Moreno when he was in Toronto for the 2001 Molson Indy. Roberto's comment? It was the best veal he'd ever had.

2	lemons, juiced		4	shallots, finely chopped
4 cloves	garlic, minced		4 cloves	garlic, minced
1/4 cup	olive oil		2 cups	sliced oyster mushrooms
2 tbsp.	chopped fresh rosemary		1 cup	sliced shiitake mushrooms
2 tbsp.	Dijon mustard		1 cup	sliced brown mushrooms
	Cracked black pepper		1 cup	sliced exotic mushrooms (chanterelles, morels, porcini or puffballs)
4	bone-in veal rack chops (each 16 oz.)		1/4 cup	port
			1/4 to 1/2 cup	veal stock
Mushroom Fricassee			2 large balls	buffalo mozzarella cheese, each cut into 4 slices
1/4 cup	olive oil			

1. In a glass dish large enough to hold the chops in one layer, whisk together the lemon juice, garlic, oil, rosemary and mustard. Season to taste with lots of pepper. Add the chops, turning to coat. Marinate, covered and refrigerated, for 4 to 6 hours.
2. To prepare the mushroom fricassee, heat the oil in a large saucepan over medium-high heat. Sauté the shallots, garlic and all of the mushrooms until tender, 8 to 10 minutes.
3. Add port and cook, stirring, for 1 minute. Stir in stock. Bring to a boil, reduce heat to low and simmer, stirring occasionally, for 10 minutes. Remove from heat and keep warm.
4. Preheat grill to medium-high.
5. Remove chops from marinade (reserving the marinade). Grill chops, basting with the marinade, for 6 to 8 minutes per side for medium-rare. When the chops are just done, move them to the side of the grill. Top each chop with one-quarter of the mushroom fricassee and 1 or 2 slices of buffalo mozzarella. Close the lid and heat until the cheese is melted and bubbling. Serve immediately.

Serves 4

Grilled Veal Liver with BBQ Sauced Bacon and Onions and Grilled Apples

When I worked at Rhodes restaurant in Toronto, one of the house specialties was grilled veal liver with bacon and onions, cooked however you liked it.

8 slices	thick-cut bacon, cut crosswise into 1/4-inch-thick strips	1 tbsp.	chopped fresh sage
			Salt and pepper to taste
1	large Spanish onion, sliced	4	Granny Smith apples
4 cloves	garlic, minced	2 tbsp.	lemon juice
1 1/2 cups	gourmet BBQ sauce	8 slices	veal liver (each 3 to 4 oz. and 1/2 inch thick)
1/4 cup	apple butter		
2 tbsp.	apple cider vinegar		Vegetable oil

1. Cook the bacon in a medium saucepan over medium-high heat, stirring, until crisp, 5 to 8 minutes. Using a slotted spoon, remove the bacon from the pot and set aside. Drain off all except 2 tbsp. of the bacon fat. Sauté the onions and garlic until the onions are tender and golden brown, 8 to 10 minutes. Stir in the BBQ sauce, apple butter, vinegar and sage. Bring to a boil, reduce heat and simmer for 5 minutes. Stir in bacon, salt and pepper. Remove from heat and keep warm.
2. Preheat grill to medium-high. Season the grill rack well (the liver tends to stick).
3. Core the apples and cut into 1/2-inch-thick rounds. Place apples in a bowl and add the lemon juice and enough water to cover. (This will prevent the apples from turning brown.)
4. Rub the liver with vegetable oil and sprinkle both sides with salt and pepper to taste.
5. Grill apple slices until lightly charred, 3 to 5 minutes per side. Season to taste with salt and pepper. Move apples to upper rack to keep warm.
6. Grill liver for 1 to 2 minutes per side for medium-rare. Be careful—and patient— when turning the liver, as it tends to stick to the grill.
7. Serve liver topped with the bacon and onions and 2 slices of grilled apple.

Serves 4

Grilled Veal Tenderloin with Horseradish Gremolata

Gremolata is a traditional garnish for veal dishes. It combines parsley, lemon zest and garlic with olive oil or melted butter. It is a tart accompaniment for succulent veal.

4	veal tenderloin fillets (each 8 oz. and 1½ inches thick)	6 cloves	garlic, minced
¼ cup	Great Canadian Steak Spice (page 98)	2	lemons, zested and juiced
	Olive oil	1 cup	chopped fresh parsley
		½ cup	freshly grated horseradish
		¼ cup	grated Parmesan cheese
Horseradish Gremolata		1 tbsp.	chopped fresh oregano
		1 tsp.	cracked black pepper
¼ cup	olive oil		Salt to taste

1. Season veal with the Steak Spice, pressing the seasoning into the meat. Brush with olive oil and set aside.
2. To make the gremolata, in a small saucepan, heat the olive oil over medium heat. Cook the garlic until tender, 1 to 2 minutes. Remove from heat and let cool slightly. Stir in the lemon zest and juice, parsley, horseradish, Parmesan cheese, oregano, pepper and salt.
3. Preheat grill to medium-high.
4. Grill veal for 3 to 4 minutes per side for medium-rare.
5. Serve each steak topped with 2 tbsp. of gremolata.

Serves 4

Grilled Chicken and Vegetable Lasagna, p. 177

Stuffed Pork Ribs with Curried Fruit Compote, p.126

Grilled T-Bone Steak with Stilton and Port Sauce, p. 152

Grilled Tuna and Vegetable Pan Bagnat, p. 84

Sticky Love Chops

This sticky, delicious sauce is modeled after Chinese orange sauce. You'll find dried orange peel in Asian food stores. Try this sauce on chicken too.

6	pork loin chops (each 6 oz. and 1 inch thick)	4	1-inch pieces dried orange peel
2 tbsp.	Miami Spice Love Paste (page 107)	4	dried whole small Asian red chilies
1/4 cup	brown sugar	3 cloves	garlic, minced
2 tbsp.	water	1 tbsp.	finely chopped fresh ginger
1/2 cup	freshly squeezed orange juice	2 tsp.	cornstarch, dissolved in 2 tbsp. water
2 tbsp.	soy sauce		Salt and pepper
3 tbsp.	butter		

1. Rub the pork chops with the Love Paste, pressing the seasoning into the meat. Marinate, covered and refrigerated, for 2 hours.
2. Meanwhile, prepare the orange sauce. Heat the sugar and water in a small heavy saucepan over medium heat, stirring occasionally with a wooden spoon, until the caramel is thick and a light golden brown. Immediately remove from heat. Whisking constantly, add the orange juice and soy sauce in a steady stream. Whisk in 2 tbsp. of the butter. Bring to a boil and simmer for 5 minutes. Remove from heat.
3. In another small saucepan, melt the remaining 1 tbsp. butter over medium-high heat. Sauté the orange peel, chilies, garlic and ginger until tender, 1 to 2 minutes. Pour in the orange sauce. Bring to a boil, reduce heat to low and simmer for 10 minutes, stirring occasionally. Season to taste with salt and pepper.
4. Stir in the cornstarch mixture. Return to a boil, reduce heat to low and simmer, stirring, until the sauce is thick, 2 to 3 minutes. Remove glaze from heat.
5. Preheat grill to medium-high.
6. Grill chops for 5 minutes. Turn them, brush with the glaze, and grill until just cooked through and the juices run clear, another 5 to 6 minutes.
7. Serve chops with remaining glaze.

Serves 6

Southwest Pork Chops with Charred Corn and Poblano Crust

Ask your butcher to prepare these thick-cut frenched pork loin chops for you. Be careful not to overcook them, or they'll be dry and tough.

4	frenched pork loin chops (each 16 oz. and 2 inches thick)	2 ears	corn, husked
¼ cup + 2 tsp.	Bone Dust BBQ Spice (page 99)	1	small red onion
		1	small white onion
		2	poblano peppers
6 cloves	garlic, chopped	8 slices	thick-cut bacon, cut crosswise into ¼-inch-thick strips
1 can	beer		
¼ cup	vegetable oil	2 tbsp.	honey
¼ cup	Dijon mustard	¼ cup	gourmet BBQ sauce
2 tbsp.	chopped fresh cilantro	1 tbsp.	hot sauce
1 tbsp.	crushed red chilies	1 tsp.	Worcestershire sauce
		4 slices	pepper Jack cheese

1. Rub the pork chops with ¼ cup of the Bone Dust BBQ Spice, pressing the seasoning into the meat. In a glass dish large enough to hold the chops in one layer, whisk together the garlic, beer, oil, mustard, cilantro and crushed chilies. Add chops, turning to coat evenly. Marinate, covered and refrigerated, for 4 to 6 hours.
2. Preheat grill to medium-high.
3. Grill the corn, red onion and white onion until lightly charred, 5 to 10 minutes. Set aside. Roast the poblano peppers, with the lid closed, until charred, 10 to 15 minutes. Peel, seed and thinly slice the poblano peppers. Thinly slice the onions. Cut kernels from the corn. Combine corn, onions and peppers in a bowl.
4. Fry the bacon until crisp. Reduce heat to low and add the grilled vegetables, honey, BBQ sauce, hot sauce, Worcestershire sauce and remaining 2 tsp. Bone Dust BBQ Spice. Mix thoroughly and cook until heated through. Remove from heat and let topping cool.

5. Preheat grill to medium-high.
6. Grill chops for 4 to 5 minutes per side. Move chops to the top rack of the grill and close the lid. Cook the chops with indirect heat until just cooked through and the juices run clear, 10 to 15 minutes.
7. Spread 1/4 cup of topping on each chop and top with a slice of cheese. Close the lid and cook until the cheese has melted.
8. Serve immediately.

Serves 4

Grilled Ham Steak with Pineapple Sauce

You can find ham steaks in most grocery stores. I look for large steaks that have a center leg bone still intact—usually a sign that the ham has not been processed too much. One steak is usually good for two to four people, but this recipe is pretty delicious so I suggest that one steak feeds two.

1	can (14 oz.) crushed pineapple, drained	2 tsp.	dry mustard
1 cup	pineapple juice	12	maraschino cherries, quartered
1/2 cup	orange marmalade	2	large smoked ham steaks (about 1 inch thick)
1/4 cup	sugar		

1. In a medium saucepan, combine the crushed pineapple, pineapple juice, marmalade, sugar and mustard. Bring to a boil, reduce heat and simmer, stirring occasionally, until thickened, about 15 minutes. Remove from heat and stir in cherries. Keep sauce warm.
2. Preheat grill to medium-high.
3. Cut the edges of the ham steak at 2-inch intervals to prevent the steaks from curling up on the grill. Grill steaks until lightly charred, 4 to 5 minutes per side.
4. Cut the steaks into 2 or 4 pieces. Serve with the sauce.

Serves 2 to 4

Grilled Butterflied Pork Tenderloin with Wasabi Teriyaki Glazing Sauce

This is a fast and easy recipe and one of my favorite pork recipes. It's all in the sauce. If you're lucky enough to have any leftovers, thinly slice them for a sandwich.

2	pork tenderloins (each 3/4 to 1 lb.)	1/2 cup	brown sugar	
1/2 cup	Bone Dust BBQ Spice (page 99)	1/4 cup	rice vinegar	
		1/4 cup	mirin (sweet rice wine) or medium-dry sherry	
Wasabi Teriyaki Glazing Sauce		1/4 cup	soy sauce	
		1/4 cup	water	
2 tbsp.	vegetable oil	1 tbsp.	prepared horseradish	
1 tsp.	sesame oil	1 tsp.	wasabi powder	
4 cloves	garlic, minced		Salt and pepper to taste	
1 tbsp.	finely chopped fresh ginger			

1. To prepare the glazing sauce, in a medium saucepan over medium-high heat, heat the vegetable oil and sesame oil. Sauté the garlic and ginger until transparent and tender, 3 to 4 minutes. Stir in the brown sugar, rice vinegar, mirin, soy sauce and water. Bring to a boil, reduce heat and simmer, stirring occasionally, for 15 minutes. Remove from heat and whisk in the horseradish, wasabi powder, salt and pepper. Let cool.

2. Trim the pork tenderloins of any excess fat and sinew. To butterfly the pork, with a sharp knife, cut along the length of the tenderloins, making a deep incision about three-quarters of the way through. Open up the tenderloins so they lie flat and place between 2 sheets of plastic wrap. Lightly pound the tenderloins with the smooth side of a meat mallet until they are 1 inch thick.

3. Rub the tenderloins with the Bone Dust BBQ Spice, pressing the seasoning into the meat. Place the tenderloins in a glass dish and pour three-quarters of the glazing sauce over the pork. (Reserve remaining sauce for glazing.) Marinate, covered and refrigerated, for 2 hours.

4. Preheat grill to medium-high.
5. Grill tenderloins, basting liberally with reserved glazing sauce, for 4 to 5 minutes per side for medium. Let tenderloins rest for 5 minutes.
6. Thinly slice tenderloins and serve glazed with remaining sauce.

Serves 6

Jerk Rotisserie of Pork Loin with Maple Jerk BBQ Sauce

While filming King of the Q *in Jamaica, I had the pleasure of preparing this dish for our first episode. This is an easy way to prepare tender succulent pork.*

1	boneless pork loin (4 to 5 lb. and 12 to 18 inches long)	
2 bottles	beer	
1 cup	Jamaican Jerk Paste (page 106)	
1/2 cup	sugar	
1/4 cup	salt	

Maple Jerk BBQ Sauce

2 1/2 cups	gourmet BBQ sauce
1/2 cup	maple syrup
1/4 cup	Jamaican Jerk Paste (page 106)
1/2 bottle	beer

1. Place the pork loin in a deep roasting pan or large resealable plastic bag.
2. Whisk together beer, Jerk Paste, sugar and salt. Pour over pork loin and marinate, covered and refrigerated, for 24 hours.
3. To prepare the sauce, whisk together the BBQ sauce, maple syrup, Jerk Paste and beer.
4. Preheat grill to high.
5. Discard the marinade and skewer the pork with the rotisserie rod. Secure the loin with the rotisserie spikes. Place pork on the rotisserie, season with salt and close the lid. Sear the meat for 15 minutes.
6. Reduce heat to medium-low and cook, basting frequently with the sauce, until a meat thermometer reads 150°F (for medium), 1 to 1 1/2 hours.
7. Remove pork from the rotisserie and carefully remove the rotisserie rod. Let meat rest for 10 minutes.
8. Give the pork a final baste and cut into 1-inch-thick slices. Serve with remaining sauce.

Serves 8

Redneck Riviera Smoked Boston Butt with Jack Daniel's BBQ Sauce

Chef Bill Hahne is the president of the Research Chefs Association in North America and is an avid meat smoker. As he says, he lives along the Redneck Riviera, a stretch of beach along the coast of Mississippi and the Gulf of Mexico. Bill has converted his beer fridge into a smoker on his front porch. (Personally, Bill, I would have gotten another fridge for the beer.)

The key to a successful smoked pork shoulder is the low and slow method of smoking. Bill adds a little twist that will ensure tender, mouth-watering pulled pork every time. Once the shoulder is cooked, he places it in the refrigerator, loosely covered, for 24 hours. Then he puts the pork in a large pot, covers it with a blend of water and Jack Daniel's and simmers it for 2 hours. The meat literally shreds off the bone, pig-pickin' style!

By the way, Boston butt is the smoker's term for pork shoulder.

1	bone-in Boston butt pork shoulder roast (7 to 9 lb.)	2 cups	Jack Daniel's Sour Mash Whiskey
1 cup	Bone Dust BBQ Spice (page 99)	3 cups	hickory smoke–flavored BBQ sauce
	Mesquite or hickory smoking chunks, soaked in water for at least 30 minutes	1/2 cup	malt vinegar
		1/4 cup	brown sugar
			Salt and pepper

1. Rub the pork with the Bone Dust BBQ Spice, pressing the seasoning into the meat.
2. Prepare your smoker according to manufacturer's instructions to a temperature of 225°F, using about 12 charcoal coals. (See page 115.) Place the pork shoulder on the top rack of the smoker and close the lid. Add soaked wood chunks to the charcoal for the first 2 hours of cooking. (I like to put the chips directly on the hot coals.)
3. Smoke the pork for 6 to 8 hours, until a meat thermometer inserted in the thickest part of the meat nearest the bone reads 180°F and when you pull on the blade bone it pulls clean from the meat. Adjust the air vents to maintain a temperature of

225°F and replenish coals and water as needed. If the meat looks dry, spray it with a little water or Jack Daniel's.

4. Transfer the pork to a bowl and loosely cover with plastic wrap. Refrigerate for at least 24 hours or up to a week.

5. Put the pork in a large pot. Add 1 cup of the Jack Daniel's and enough water to cover. Bring to a boil, reduce heat to low and simmer for 2 hours.

6. Meanwhile, prepare the sauce. Whisk together the remaining 1 cup Jack Daniel's, the BBQ sauce, vinegar and brown sugar.

7. Remove pork from the pot and let rest for 10 minutes. Using a fork or your hands, shred the meat from the bone into small strips. Place meat in a large bowl and add the sauce a little at a time, mixing thoroughly. Season to taste with salt and pepper. Some like their pulled pork dry and others like it saucy.

8. Serve pulled pork piled high on fresh buns.

Serves 10 to 12

Luau Stuffed Leg of Lamb

Treat the macadamia nuts like gold; they're expensive and delicious. If you want, substitute pecans.

2	red chilies, finely chopped	1/4 cup	melted butter
6 cloves	garlic, minced	1	boneless leg of lamb (4 to 5 lb.), butterflied
4	green onions, finely chopped		
2 cups	diced fresh pineapple	1/4 cup	Bone Dust BBQ Spice (page 99)
1/2 cup	chopped macadamia nuts		
1/2 cup	fresh bread crumbs		
2 tbsp.	curry paste		***Honey Mustard Baste***
1 tbsp.	finely chopped fresh ginger	1/2 cup	butter
1 tbsp.	chopped fresh parsley	1/2 cup	honey
1/2 cup	pineapple juice	1/2 cup	pineapple juice

1. To prepare the baste, in a small saucepan, melt the butter over medium heat. Whisk in the honey and pineapple juice until fully incorporated. Set aside.
2. In a bowl, combine the chilies, garlic, green onions, pineapple, macadamia nuts, bread crumbs, curry paste, ginger and parsley. Add the pineapple juice and melted butter a little at a time, stirring to incorporate. The stuffing should be a little moist.
3. Open up the butterflied lamb leg and rub with the Bone Dust BBQ Spice, pressing the seasoning into the meat. Spread the stuffing evenly over the inside of the lamb leg.
4. Starting from the wide end, roll up the leg. Tie securely with string.
5. Preheat grill to high.
6. Insert the rotisserie rod and place the lamb on the grill. Sear the lamb for 8 to 10 minutes. Reduce heat to medium and continue to roast, brushing occasionally with the baste, until a meat thermometer reads 140 to 145°F (for medium), 60 to 70 minutes. Remove lamb from grill and let rest for 5 minutes.
7. Thinly slice and serve.

Serves 8

Lamb Loin Chops with Pecan Goat Cheese

I first made this recipe on the set of King of the Q, *and since then it has become a barbecue favorite at my home. Tender lamb chops don't need to marinate. Just season, grill, baste and consume.*

12	lamb loin chops (each about 2 inches thick)	1 tbsp.	chopped fresh rosemary
		1 tbsp.	Worcestershire sauce
1/4 cup	Great Canadian Steak Spice (page 98)		Salt and pepper
8 cloves	garlic, minced	1/2 cup	coarsely crushed smoked pecans
1/2 cup	steak sauce	1/2 cup	creamy goat cheese
1/4 cup	ketchup	1/4 cup	butter, softened
1/4 cup	honey		

1. Rub the chops with the Steak Spice, pressing the seasoning into the meat.
2. In a bowl whisk together the garlic, steak sauce, ketchup, honey, rosemary and Worcestershire sauce. Season to taste with salt and pepper.
3. In another bowl, combine the pecans, goat cheese and butter.
4. Preheat grill to medium-high.
5. Grill chops, basting liberally with the sauce, for 6 to 8 minutes per side for medium-rare.
6. Serve chops topped with a dollop of pecan goat cheese.

Serves 4

Hot and Spicy Grilled Rack of Lamb

I like to use large racks of lamb from Canada, the U.S. or Australia. I find that these racks tend to have a little more meat as well as a nice amount of marbling and external fat, which add great flavor to a very simple grilling dish.

2	frenched lamb racks (each 1½ lb.)	3	red finger chili peppers, thinly sliced
¼ cup	Licorice Rub (page 108)	½ cup	stem ginger or orange marmalade
2 tbsp.	vegetable oil	¼ cup	apple juice
2 cloves	garlic, minced	1 tbsp.	chopped fresh cilantro
4	jalapeño peppers, seeded and thinly sliced	1	lime, juiced
			Salt and pepper

1. Rub the lamb racks with the Licorice Rub, pressing the seasoning into the meat. Cover and marinate at room temperature for 1 hour.
2. Heat the oil in a medium saucepan over medium heat. Sauté the garlic, jalapeño and chili peppers until tender, 2 to 3 minutes. Stir in the marmalade and apple juice. Bring to a low boil, reduce heat to low and simmer for 10 minutes, stirring occasionally. Stir in the cilantro and lime juice. Season to taste with salt and pepper. Remove sauce from heat and set aside.
3. Preheat grill to medium-high.
4. Sear lamb for 2 to 3 minutes per side. Move lamb to the top rack for indirect cooking. Reduce heat to medium and close the lid. Grill-roast, basting occasionally with the sauce, for 12 to 15 minutes for medium-rare. Remove lamb from grill and let rest for 5 minutes.
5. Slice between every rib bone and serve with reheated remaining sauce.

Serves 4

Grilled Venison Rack Chops with Smoked Chocolate and Poblano Chili Sauce

Yes, you read this correctly—smoked chocolate with venison. Trust me, the rich flavor of the venison blends magnificently with the buttery smoked chocolate.

2	frenched venison racks (each with 8 ribs)	1 cup	heavy cream
1/4 cup	Bone Dust BBQ Spice (page 99)	1/4 cup	cognac
		1 cup	smoked bittersweet chocolate (page 222), coarsely chopped
2 tbsp.	butter		
2 cloves	garlic, minced	1 tbsp.	chopped fresh savory
1	shallot, finely chopped		Salt and pepper to taste
2	poblano peppers, roasted, peeled, seeded and cut into 1-inch strips		

1. Rub the venison with the Bone Dust BBQ Spice, pressing the seasoning into the meat.
2. Melt the butter in a small saucepan over medium-high heat. Sauté the garlic and shallot until tender, 1 to 2 minutes. Add the poblano peppers, cream and cognac. Bring to a boil and reduce heat. Stirring constantly, add the chocolate a little at a time until melted. Simmer gently until thick, about 5 minutes. Stir in savory, salt and pepper. Remove sauce from heat and keep warm.
3. Preheat grill to medium-high.
4. Grill racks for 7 to 10 minutes per side for medium-rare. Remove racks from grill and let rest for 5 minutes.
5. Cut each rack into 4 thick chops and spoon chocolate sauce over each chop.

Serves 8

Hot-Buttered Breasts and Thighs

Chicken

Cornish Hen

Turkey

Quail

Duck

Smoked Maple Bourbon Glazed Chicken Halves

Grill-roasted half chickens are a sticky feast when the glaze is made with bourbon and maple syrup—a combination that is hard not to drink.

2	chickens (each 3 to 4 lb.)	1/2 cup	maple syrup
1/2 cup	Hell's Fire Chili Paste (page 102)	1/4 cup	brown sugar
		1/4 cup	bourbon
	Mesquite smoking chips or chunks	1/4 cup	orange juice
			Salt and pepper to taste

1. Using a pair of poultry or kitchen shears, cut along each side of the backbone. Using a sharp knife, cut through the breast bone to separate the chickens into two halves. Rub with the Hell's Fire Paste, pressing the seasoning into the skin and meat.
2. Prepare your smoker according to manufacturer's instructions to a temperature of 225°F. (See page 115.) Add soaked mesquite smoking chips.
3. Place chicken skin side up on smoking rack and close the lid. Smoke chickens until fully cooked (a meat thermometer will read 180°F), 4 to 6 hours, replenishing smoking chips, coals and water as required.
4. Meanwhile, prepare the glaze. In a large bowl, whisk together the maple syrup, brown sugar, bourbon, orange juice, salt and pepper.
5. Preheat grill to medium.
6. Place chickens on grill bone side down. Close the lid and grill-roast, basting with the glaze, until the skin is crisp and the chicken hot, 5 to 10 minutes.
7. Serve with remaining glaze.

Serves 4

Grilled Chicken and Vegetable Lasagna

I have never been a fan of lasagna. Its not that lasagna is not good but I am just not a fan of tomato sauce and cheese. My Pamela has requested me to make lasagna on many occasions and I have not obliged until now. I made this version of the classic on a grill and with a cream sauce instead. It is rich and decadent and has a ton of cheese. Enjoy!

4	boneless, skinless chicken breasts (each 6 oz.)
2 tbsp.	Bone Dust BBQ Spice (page 99)
1/4 cup + 2 tbsp.	vegetable oil
4	Portobello mushroom caps
2	zucchini, cut in half lengthwise
2	red bell peppers, halved lengthwise
1	eggplant, sliced lengthwise 1/4 inch thick
1	fennel bulb, halved lengthwise
1	large Spanish onion, sliced into 1/2-inch-thick rounds
1/4 cup	balsamic vinegar
	Salt and pepper to taste

3 cloves	garlic, minced
2 tbsp.	chopped fresh herbs
4 cups	shredded mozzarella cheese
2 cups	shredded Friulano or provolone cheese
1/4 cup	dry bread crumbs
6 sheets	fresh pasta (8 x 10 inches)

Parmesan Cream Sauce

4 tbsp.	butter
2 cloves	garlic, minced
5 tbsp.	all-purpose flour
4 cups	chicken stock
1 cup	grated Parmesan cheese
1 cup	heavy cream
1 tsp.	Worcestershire sauce
	Salt and pepper to taste
2 cups	ricotta cheese

1. Preheat grill to medium-high.
2. Rub the chicken with the Bone Dust BBQ Spice, pressing the seasoning into the meat and skin. Rub with 2 tbsp. of the oil.
3. In a large bowl, combine the mushroom caps, zucchini, red peppers, eggplant, fennel, onion, remaining 1/4 cup oil, the vinegar, salt and pepper. Toss well.
4. Grill chicken until fully cooked, 5 to 6 minutes per side. Let cool.

5. Grill vegetables, turning occasionally, until just cooked and slightly charred, 15 to 20 minutes. Let cool.

6. To prepare the cream sauce, melt the butter in a medium saucepan over medium-high heat. Sauté the garlic until tender, about 2 minutes. Add the flour, stirring constantly until fully mixed, being careful not to burn. Whisking constantly, add the stock a little at a time until fully incorporated. Bring to boil, reduce heat to low and simmer, stirring occasionally, until fairly thick, about 20 minutes. Whisk in Parmesan, cream, Worcestershire sauce, salt and pepper. Let cool. When the sauce has cooled, whisk in the ricotta cheese.

7. Preheat oven to 375°F. Spray a 10- × 8- × 3-inch lasagna pan with nonstick cooking spray.

8. Cut the chicken and vegetables into 1/2-inch-thick slices and toss with the garlic and herbs.

9. Combine the mozzarella and Friulano cheeses.

10. Sprinkle the lasagna pan with the bread crumbs. Spread 1/2 cup of the cream sauce evenly in the pan. Lay 2 pasta sheets over the sauce. Spread half of the chicken mixture evenly over the pasta. Spread 1 cup of the sauce over the chicken mixture. Top with 2 cups of the cheese. Lay 2 more sheets of pasta over the cheese. Top with remaining chicken mixture, 1 cup of sauce and 2 cups of cheese. Finish with 2 more sheets of pasta, the remaining sauce and remaining cheese.

11. Bake, uncovered, until the corners are bubbling and the top is golden brown, about 1 1/2 hours.

12. Let rest for 10 minutes before serving.

Serves 8

Grilled Chicken Breasts Stuffed with Peaches, Brie and Shrimp

For this recipe it is easiest if you buy hotel-style chicken breasts suprêmes. These are large skin-on boneless chicken breasts (about 6 to 8 oz. each) with the wing drumstick attached. Ask your butcher to prepare these breasts for you.

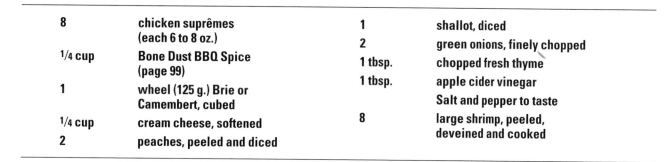

8	chicken suprêmes (each 6 to 8 oz.)	1	shallot, diced
1/4 cup	Bone Dust BBQ Spice (page 99)	2	green onions, finely chopped
		1 tbsp.	chopped fresh thyme
1	wheel (125 g.) Brie or Camembert, cubed	1 tbsp.	apple cider vinegar
			Salt and pepper to taste
1/4 cup	cream cheese, softened	8	large shrimp, peeled, deveined and cooked
2	peaches, peeled and diced		

1. Cut the tenderloins from the breasts. Place tenderloins between 2 sheets of plastic wrap and gently flatten with the smooth side of a meat mallet. Set aside.
2. Using a sharp knife, cut an incision down the center of the breast about 1/2 inch deep. With the tip of the knife, make an angled cut on each side of the initial cut into but not all the way through the breast. With your fingers, push the meat aside to make a large pocket. Season the chicken inside and out with the Bone Dust BBQ Spice.
3. In a food processor, blend the Brie and cream cheese. Transfer mixture to a bowl and stir in the peaches, shallot, green onions, thyme, vinegar, salt and pepper.
4. Divide the brie stuffing into 8 equal portions. Place a portion of stuffing in the palm of your hand. Press 1 shrimp into the stuffing. Mold the stuffing around the shrimp to encase it. Place the stuffing in a chicken pocket and press firmly to slightly flatten.
5. Place a tenderloin over the stuffing and tuck the edges into the pocket. Firmly press the edges together to make a tight seal. Repeat with remaining breasts.
6. Preheat grill to medium-high.
7. Grill chickens, starting skin side down, until fully cooked, 6 to 8 minutes per side.
8. Serve immediately.

Serves 8

Chinese Lemon Grilled Chicken Breasts

You know your favorite Chinese restaurant that serves that tangy lemon chicken? Well, I think I've captured that wonderful flavor for you. Lots of fresh lemon juice adds zing in this recipe.

6	boneless, skinless chicken breasts	1/4 cup	sugar
2 tbsp.	Indonesian Cinnamon Rub (page 105)	1/4 cup	pineapple juice
		1 tbsp.	rice vinegar
3	lemons, zested and juiced	2 tsp.	crushed red chilies
3 cloves	garlic, minced	2 tsp.	cornstarch, dissolved in 2 tbsp. water
1 tbsp.	finely chopped fresh ginger		
1 tbsp.	vegetable oil	2	green onions, finely chopped
2 tsp.	sesame oil		Salt and pepper

1. Rub the chicken with the Cinnamon Rub, pressing the seasoning into the meat.
2. In a glass dish large enough to hold the chicken in one layer, whisk together 1/4 cup of the lemon juice, the garlic, ginger, vegetable oil and sesame oil. Add chicken, turning to coat. Marinate, covered and refrigerated, for 4 to 6 hours.
3. In a medium saucepan, combine the remaining lemon juice, the lemon zest, sugar, pineapple juice, vinegar and crushed chilies. Bring to a low boil. Stir in the cornstarch mixture. Reduce heat and simmer, stirring, until thickened. Remove from heat and stir in green onions. Season sauce to taste with salt and pepper.
4. Preheat grill to medium-high.
5. Grill chicken, basting with the sauce, until golden brown and fully cooked, 5 to 6 minutes per side.
6. Serve immediately with remaining warmed sauce.

Serves 6

Hot Buttered Love Chicken Thighs with Honey Butter

The best cut of chicken for me is the underrated thigh. Not only is the thigh inexpensive but it has more flavor and succulence than any other part of the chicken. Slowly grill-roast these thighs, basting them lusciously with the honey butter glazing sauce.

12	chicken thighs	1/2 cup	honey
1/4 cup	Indonesian Cinnamon Rub (page 105)	1/4 cup	lemon juice
1/2 lb. + 1 tbsp.	cold butter (1/2 lb. cubed)	1 tbsp.	chopped fresh sage
8 cloves	garlic, minced	1 tbsp.	curry paste
1 tbsp.	finely chopped fresh ginger		Salt and pepper

1. Rub the chicken with the Cinnamon Rub, pressing the seasoning into the meat and skin. Set aside.
2. To prepare the glazing sauce, melt 1 tbsp. of the butter in a medium saucepan over medium heat. Sauté the garlic and ginger until tender, 2 to 3 minutes. Add the honey, lemon juice, sage and curry paste, stirring until fully incorporated. Slowly bring to a boil and remove from heat. Whisk in the cubed butter a little at a time until fully incorporated. Season to taste with salt and pepper.
3. Preheat grill to medium-high.
4. Sear chicken for 2 to 3 minutes per side and move to a cooler part of the grill. Close the lid and grill-roast the thighs, basting every 10 minutes with lots of the glazing sauce, until fully cooked, 20 to 30 minutes. Move chicken directly over heat source and grill for 1 to 2 minutes more to crisp the skin.
5. Baste once again and serve.

Serves 6

BBQ Chicken Steaks

What is a chicken steak? Simply put, it's a butterflied boneless chicken thigh. You can leave the skin on for added flavor or remove it for a leaner recipe.

12	boneless chicken thighs	1/4 cup	corn syrup
1/4 cup	Bone Dust BBQ Spice (page 99)	1/4 cup	ketchup
		1/4 cup	steak sauce
4 cloves	garlic, minced	1 tbsp.	chopped fresh rosemary
1	small onion, finely chopped	1 tbsp.	Worcestershire sauce
3/4 cup	gourmet BBQ sauce	1 tbsp.	cracked black pepper

1. Soak 24 bamboo skewers (6 to 8 inches) in warm water for 1 hour. (Or use metal skewers.)
2. Rub the chicken with the Bone Dust BBQ Spice, pressing the seasoning into the meat. Skewer each thigh with 2 skewers in an X pattern. (This will keep the chicken flat during grilling.)
3. In a medium saucepan over medium heat, combine the garlic, onion, BBQ sauce, corn syrup, ketchup, steak sauce, rosemary, Worcestershire sauce and pepper. Slowly bring to a boil, stirring occasionally. Simmer for 10 minutes. Remove sauce from heat.
4. Preheat grill to medium-high.
5. Grill chicken, basting with the sauce, until fully cooked and slightly charred, 5 to 6 minutes per side.

Serves 6

Bacon-Wrapped BBQ Drumsticks

Bacon should be its own food group. It just makes things taste better. And wrapped around these drumsticks, it also makes everything look better.

12	chicken drumsticks or thighs	1¹/2 cups	ketchup
¹/4 cup	Bone Dust BBQ Spice (page 99)	¹/2 cup	maple syrup
		2 tbsp.	lemon juice
12 slices	bacon	1 tbsp.	chopped fresh thyme
	Whole cloves	1 tbsp.	Worcestershire sauce
4 cloves	garlic, minced		Salt and pepper

1. Rub chicken pieces with Bone Dust BBQ Spice, pressing the seasoning into the meat and skin. Roll a slice of bacon around each piece of chicken and fasten with a tooth-pick. Stick 1 or 2 whole cloves into each piece of chicken.
2. In a bowl, whisk together the garlic, ketchup, maple syrup, lemon juice, thyme and Worcestershire sauce. Season sauce to taste with salt and pepper.
3. Preheat grill to medium.
4. Place chicken in a grill basket. Grill chicken, basting liberally with the sauce, until fully cooked and the bacon is crisp, 10 to 12 minutes per side. (If the bacon causes a flare-up, move chicken to the cooler side of grill and cook indirectly.)
5. Carefully remove chicken from grill basket and toss in remaining sauce.
6. Serve immediately or cool thoroughly and place in an airtight container for a picnic.

Serves 6

Grilled Butterflied Cornish Hens with Hard Lemonade Glazing Sauce

On a hot summer's day nothing is more refreshing to drink than one of those hard lemonade coolers. And here's a recipe where you can eat it too.

If you don't want to do it yourself, have your butcher remove the thigh bones, back bone and rib cage from the Cornish hens.

4	Cornish game hens	2 tbsp.	chopped fresh sage
1/4 cup	Herb Mustard Rub (page 104)	1 tbsp.	cracked black pepper
2	lemons, thinly sliced	2 cans	hard lemonade
8 cloves	garlic, minced	1/4 cup	honey
1	onion, thinly sliced	2 tbsp.	cold butter
1/4 cup	olive oil		Salt to taste

1. Soak 8 bamboo skewers (7 to 10 inches) in water for 15 minutes. (Or use metal skewers.)
2. Rinse and pat dry the game hens. Using a pair of poultry or kitchen shears, cut along each side of the backbone. Using a sharp knife, carefully remove the rib cage, breast bone and leg bones. Rub hens with the Herb Mustard Rub, pressing the seasoning into the skin and meat.
3. Place the hens skin side up and bring the legs up snugly to the body. Skewer each hen in an "X" pattern, starting by inserting a skewer through one leg and through the opposite breast, exiting near the wing. Repeat on the other side.
4. In a bowl, combine the lemon slices, garlic, onion, olive oil, sage, pepper and 1 1/2 cans of the hard lemonade. Pour half of the marinade into a glass dish large enough to hold the hens. Place the hens on top and cover with remaining marinade. Marinate, covered and refrigerated, for 2 hours.
5. Meanwhile, in a small saucepan over medium heat, whisk together the remaining 1/2 can of hard lemonade (that is, if you haven't drunk it yet) and the honey. When hot, whisk in the butter until fully incorporated. Remove glazing sauce from heat.

6. Preheat grill to medium-high.
7. Remove hens from marinade and season with salt. Grill hens, starting with skin side down and basting with glazing sauce, until fully cooked and crisp, 6 to 8 minutes per side.
8. Serve immediately.

Serves 4

Rotisserie Turkey Breasts with Oyster Cornbread Stuffing

If you ask your butcher to get you small turkey suprêmes (boneless, skin-on breasts), this recipe won't take as long. If you want, you can also use large chicken breasts. You'll need a grill rotisserie basket for this recipe.

4	turkey breasts (each 12 to 16 oz.)	1 stalk	celery, diced
1/4 cup	Bone Dust BBQ Spice (page 99)	4 cloves	garlic, minced
		2 to 3 cups	dry cornbread cubes
2 tbsp.	butter	1/4 cup	melted butter
1 dozen	fresh oysters, shucked and liquor reserved	1/4 bottle	honey brown lager
		1 tbsp.	chopped fresh sage
4 slices	thick-cut bacon, diced		Salt and pepper
1	small onion, diced		Your favorite spicy BBQ sauce

1. Cut the tenderloins from the breasts. Place tenderloins between 2 sheets of plastic wrap and gently flatten with the smooth side of a meat mallet. Set aside.
2. Using a sharp knife, cut an incision down the center of the breast about 1/2 inch deep. With the tip of the knife, make an angled cut on each side of the initial cut into but not all the way through the breast. With your fingers, push the meat aside to make a large pocket. Season the turkey inside and out with the Bone Dust BBQ Spice.
3. In large saucepan, melt 2 tbsp. of butter over medium heat. Lightly fry the oysters until they are just firm. Using a slotted spoon, transfer the oysters to paper towels to drain.
4. Add the bacon to the pan and fry until crisp. Drain off all but 2 tbsp. of the fat. Add onion, celery and garlic; sauté for 4 to 5 minutes. Add the reserved oyster liquor, the cornbread, melted butter, beer and sage. The stuffing should be moist but not too wet, and just a little sticky. Season to taste with salt and pepper. Let cool. Fold in the oysters.

5. Divide stuffing into 4 equal portions. Place stuffing in each turkey pocket, pressing firmly to tightly pack the cavity. Place a tenderloin over the stuffing and tuck the edges into the pocket. Firmly press the edges together to make a tight seal. Repeat with remaining breasts.
6. Set up grill rotisserie according to manufacturer's instructions. Preheat grill to high (400°F).
7. Place turkey breasts in a grill rotisserie basket and secure mesh lid. Insert grill rod through basket. Grill turkey, basting lightly with BBQ sauce, until fully cooked (a meat thermometer will read 180°F), 25 to 30 minutes.
8. Cut breasts in half and serve immediately.

Serves 8

Grilled Turkey Steaks with Apple Cream Sauce

Turkey steaks are cut from a boneless, skinless breast.

8	turkey steaks (each 6 oz. and about 1 inch thick)
1/4 cup	Herb Mustard Rub (page 104)
1 cup	ranch dressing
2 tbsp.	cracked black peppercorns
2 tbsp.	vegetable oil

Apple Cream Sauce

2 tbsp.	butter
1	small yellow onion, sliced
2	green apples, thinly sliced
1/4 cup	golden raisins
2 tbsp.	apple brandy
1/2 cup	heavy cream
1/4 cup	honey
1/4 cup	ranch dressing
	Salt and pepper

1. Rub the turkey with the Herb Mustard Rub, pressing the seasoning into the meat. In a glass dish large enough to hold the turkey in one layer, whisk together the ranch dressing, peppercorns and oil. Add turkey, turning to coat. Marinate, covered and refrigerated, for 4 hours.
2. To prepare the sauce, melt the butter in a medium saucepan over medium-high heat. Sauté the onion until tender, 2 to 3 minutes. Stir in the apples and raisins; sauté for 4 to 5 minutes, stirring gently.
3. Add the apple brandy, scraping up any brown bits. Stir in the cream, honey and ranch dressing. Bring to a low boil, reduce heat and simmer until the sauce is thickened, 4 to 5 minutes. Season to taste with salt and pepper. Remove from heat and keep warm.
4. Preheat grill to medium-high.
5. Grill turkey until fully cooked, 4 to 5 minutes per side.
6. Serve immediately with the sauce.

Serves 8

Southern Comfort BBQ Quail

Southern Comfort is a liqueur made with bourbon and peaches. Another great thing to do with Southern Comfort is use it as a baste for your favorite belle or beau.
Ask your butcher to butterfly and remove the backbone and rib cage of the quail.

12	butterflied boneless quail	1/4 cup	maple syrup
1/4 cup	Bone Dust BBQ Spice (page 99)	1 tbsp.	cracked black pepper
		1 tbsp.	chopped fresh lemon thyme
	Olive oil	2 tbsp.	butter
3/4 cup	gourmet BBQ sauce	Pinch	cayenne pepper
1/4 cup	Southern Comfort		Salt to taste

1. Soak 24 bamboo skewers (about 7 inches) in water for 15 minutes. (Or use metal skewers.)
2. Rub the quail with the Bone Dust BBQ Spice, pressing the seasoning into the flesh.
3. Place the quail skin side up and bring the legs up snugly to the body. Skewer each quail in an "X" pattern, starting by inserting a skewer through one leg, under the leg bone and through the opposite breast, exiting near the wing. Repeat on the other side. Brush each quail with a little olive oil and set aside.
4. In a small saucepan over medium-high heat, whisk together the BBQ sauce, Southern Comfort, maple syrup, pepper and thyme. Bring to a low boil, stirring constantly. Remove from heat and whisk in the butter, cayenne and salt. Keep the sauce warm.
5. Preheat grill to medium-high. Grill quail skin side down for 2 to 3 minutes. Turn and continue to cook, basting with the sauce, for another 2 to 3 minutes.
6. Serve immediately.

Serves 6

Grilled Duck Breasts
with Balsamic Fig Glazing Sauce

Duck breasts are high in fat and tend to flare up on the grill. Sear them quickly on the skin side and then continue to cook them indirectly to reduce flare-ups. I recommend keeping the lid open and staying by the grill for the entire cooking time.

4	boneless duck breasts (each 8 to 12 oz.)		1 cup	balsamic vinegar
			2 tbsp.	olive oil
1/4 cup	Malabar Pepper Rub (page 96)		4 cloves	garlic, minced
			2	large shallots, finely chopped
1/4 cup	balsamic vinegar			
1/2 cup	apple juice		1/2 cup	honey
2 tbsp.	vegetable oil		1/4 cup	water
1 tbsp.	chopped fresh thyme		1 tbsp.	chopped fresh thyme
			1	vanilla bean, split
Balsamic Fig Glazing Sauce			Pinch	nutmeg
6	dried figs, coarsely chopped		1/2 cup	pecan halves, toasted and coarsely chopped
1/4 cup	amaretto			

1. Using a sharp knife, score the skin side of the duck breasts in a diamond pattern, slicing about 1/4 inch deep into the fat. Season the duck with the Pepper Rub, pressing the seasoning into the meat.
2. In a glass dish large enough to hold the duck in one layer, whisk together 1/4 cup of the balsamic vinegar, the apple juice, vegetable oil and thyme. Add the duck, turning to coat. Marinate, covered and refrigerated, for 4 hours.
3. Meanwhile, in a small bowl, soak the figs in amaretto for 1 hour.
4. In a small, heavy saucepan, bring 1 cup of balsamic vinegar to a boil; reduce by half. Remove from heat.
5. Heat the olive oil in a medium saucepan over medium-high heat. Sauté the garlic and shallots until tender, 2 to 3 minutes. Add the reduced balsamic vinegar, the figs and amaretto, the honey, water, thyme, vanilla bean and nutmeg. Bring to a

boil, reduce heat to low and simmer for 15 minutes, stirring occasionally. Remove glazing sauce from heat; discard vanilla bean. Using a hand blender, purée sauce until smooth.

6. Preheat the grill to medium-high.

7. Grill the duck, skin side down, until the skin is golden brown and crisp, 4 to 6 minutes. (If flare-ups occur, reduce grill heat and move duck so it is not directly over the flames.) Turn the duck and grill, basting with the glazing sauce, for 5 to 8 minutes for medium-rare. The duck should be golden brown and firm to the touch.

8. Remove duck from the grill and thinly slice each breast across the grain. Serve topped with the pecans and remaining glaze.

Serves 4 to 6

Smoked Peking Duck

Patience is the key to smoking—along with a few beers. Enjoy a few cold brews while tending to your duck.

You'll find Chinese crêpes in the freezer section of Asian grocery stores.

1	duck (4 to 5 lb.)		
3 tbsp.	Indonesian Cinnamon Rub (page 105)		
2	star anise		
1	cinnamon stick		
1	orange, peeled and sliced crosswise		
	Cherry smoking chips or chunks		
	Chinese crêpes		
	Thinly sliced green onions		

Peking Sauce

1 tbsp.	vegetable oil
2 tsp.	sesame oil
4 cloves	garlic, minced
1 tbsp.	finely chopped fresh ginger
1 tsp.	crushed red chilies
2	oranges, juiced
1 cup	plum sauce
1/2 cup	hoisin sauce
1/4 cup	brown sugar
1/4 cup	mirin (sweet rice wine)
3 tbsp.	soy sauce
2 tbsp.	rice vinegar
	Salt and pepper

1. Rinse the duck inside and out and pat dry. Rub the duck all over with the Cinnamon Rub, pressing the seasoning into the meat and skin. Place the star anise, cinnamon stick and orange slices inside the duck.
2. Prepare your smoker according to manufacturer's instructions to a temperature of 225°F. (See page 115.) Add soaked cherry smoking chips.
3. Place the duck on smoking rack and close the lid. Smoke duck until fully cooked (a meat thermometer will read 180°F), 4 to 6 hours. Replenish smoking chips, coals and water as required.
4. Meanwhile, prepare the sauce. Heat the vegetable oil and sesame oil in a medium saucepan over medium-high heat. Sauté the garlic, ginger and crushed chilies until the garlic is tender, 2 to 3 minutes. Add the orange juice, plum sauce, hoisin, brown sugar, mirin, soy sauce and rice vinegar; bring to a boil, stirring. Remove from heat and season to taste with salt and pepper. Set aside.

5. Preheat grill to medium-low.
6. Cut smoked duck in half. Place duck on grill bone side down and close the lid. Grill-roast until the skin is crisp and the duck hot, 5 to 10 minutes.
7. Cut duck into 4 portions and serve with warmed sauce, Chinese crêpes and green onions.

Serves 4

Sizzling Seafood

Shellfish

Squid

Frogs' Legs

Hot Smoked Halibut

Smoked halibut is also great in soups and chowders. And I like to fold it into creamy mashed potatoes.

2	halibut fillets (each 12 oz. and 1½ inches thick)	2 tbsp.	sugar
		2 tbsp.	vegetable oil
2 tbsp.	Bone Dust BBQ Spice (page 99)	¼ cup	melted butter
		¼ cup	gourmet BBQ sauce
¼ cup	apple cider vinegar	1 tbsp.	apple butter
¼ cup	apple juice		Hickory smoking chips

1. Rub the halibut with the Bone Dust BBQ Spice, pressing the seasoning into the flesh. In a glass dish large enough to hold the halibut in one layer, whisk together the vinegar, apple juice, sugar and oil. Add halibut, turning to coat. Marinate for 30 minutes.
2. Meanwhile, in a small bowl, whisk together the melted butter, BBQ sauce and apple butter.
3. Prepare your smoker according to manufacturer's instructions to a temperature of 225°F. (See page 115.) Add hickory smoking chips.
4. Place halibut on the top smoking rack. Baste with apple butter baste and close the lid. Smoke halibut for 1½ to 2½ hours, replenishing smoking chips, coals and water as required. The halibut is cooked when it easily flakes with a fork.
5. Carefully transfer halibut to a serving platter and cut each fillet in half.
6. Serve immediately with tartar sauce and grilled bread.

Serves 4

Grilled Monster Halibut Steak with Pernod Mustard Mop and Pernod Butter

Be patient when grilling this big steak, and do not turn it too often. A "mop" is a thin BBQ sauce that is basted liberally on food.

1	monster halibut steak (1¹/₂ to 2 lb. and 1¹/₂ inches thick)
3 tbsp.	Great Canadian Steak Spice (page 98)
	Olive oil, for brushing

Pernod Mustard Mop

2	shallots, finely chopped
¹/₄ cup	melted butter
¹/₄ cup	corn syrup
¹/₄ cup	Dijon mustard
¹/₄ cup	grainy mustard

¹/₄ cup	Pernod
2 tbsp.	white wine vinegar
1 tbsp.	chopped fresh tarragon
1 tbsp.	cracked black pepper
1 tsp.	dry mustard
	Salt to taste

Pernod Butter

¹/₄ lb.	butter, softened
2 tbsp.	Pernod
1 tbsp.	chopped fresh thyme
1 tsp.	cracked black pepper
Pinch	salt

1. Rub Steak Spice into halibut flesh. Brush with olive oil. Set aside.
2. To prepare the mustard mop, in a bowl whisk together the shallots, melted butter, corn syrup, Dijon mustard, grainy mustard, Pernod, vinegar, tarragon, pepper, dry mustard and salt. Set aside.
3. To prepare the Pernod butter, in a small bowl combine the butter, Pernod, thyme, pepper and salt. Cover and refrigerate until needed.
4. Preheat grill to medium-high.
5. Place halibut on a well-oiled grill topper. Grill, basting frequently with the mustard mop, until the center bone of the halibut can be pulled cleanly from the flesh, 12 to 15 minutes per side (8 to 10 minutes per inch of thickness). Remove halibut from the grill and cut into 4 portions. Serve topped with a dollop of Pernod butter.

Serves 4

Banana Leaf–Wrapped Mahi Mahi with Tropical Fruits

While in Jamaica filming King of the Q, *I had the opportunity to do a little deep-sea fishing. I caught a 25-lb., 44-inch-long mahi mahi. It was delicious, so fresh and full of flavor. Mahi mahi is a firm-fleshed fish, which makes it great for the grill. If you can't find mahi mahi, use grouper, halibut, sea bass or red snapper.*

You can find banana leaves in Asian and West Indian markets.

6	skinless mahi mahi fillets (each 6 oz. and 1 inch thick)	1 cup	diced fresh mango
3 tbsp.	Bone Dust BBQ Spice (page 99)	1 cup	diced fresh pineapple
		1 tbsp.	chopped fresh parsley
1	seedless orange, peeled and segmented	1 tbsp.	finely chopped fresh ginger
		1 tbsp.	curry paste
1	small red onion, diced		Salt and pepper to taste
1	red bell pepper, diced	2	large banana leaves
		6 tbsp.	cold butter

1. Season the mahi mahi with the Bone Dust BBQ Spice, pressing the seasoning into the flesh.
2. In a bowl, combine the orange segments, onion, red pepper, mango, pineapple, parsley, ginger, curry paste, salt and pepper.
3. Cut the banana leaves into six 12-inch squares. Place a spoonful of fruit mixture in the middle of each square. Place 1 fillet on the fruit; top each with 1 tbsp. of butter and another spoonful of fruit mixture. Fold up the bottom of the leaf, fold in the sides and fold down the top; press firmly to seal the packages. Tie each with string.
4. Preheat grill to medium-high.
5. Grill bundles, turning once, for 6 to 8 minutes per side.
6. Let rest for 3 minutes.
7. Carefully unwrap bundles and serve immediately.

Serves 6

Smoked Marlin Steak with Bacon Aïoli

Heavenly is all I can say!

2	marlin steaks (each 8 to 10 oz. and 1¹/₂ inches thick)
¹/₄ cup	Great Canadian Steak Spice (page 98)
1 tbsp.	crushed red chilies
¹/₄ cup	olive oil
	Cherry or apple smoking chips

Bacon Aïoli

2 slices	bacon, diced and fried crisp
1 clove	garlic, minced
¹/₂ cup	mayonnaise
¹/₄ cup	sour cream
2 tbsp.	lemon juice
1 tbsp.	chopped fresh dill
Dash	hot sauce
	Salt and pepper to taste

1. Rub the marlin with the Steak Spice and crushed chilies, pressing the seasoning into the flesh. Brush with olive oil and set aside.
2. To prepare the aïoli, in a bowl combine the bacon, garlic, mayonnaise, sour cream, lemon juice, dill, hot sauce, salt and pepper.
3. Prepare your smoker according to manufacturer's instructions to a temperature of 175°F. (See page 115.) Add soaked cherry smoking chips.
4. Place marlin on top rack of smoker and close the lid. Smoke for 45 to 60 minutes for medium doneness, replenishing smoking chips, coals and water as required.
5. Thinly slice marlin and serve hot or cooled with bacon aïoli.

Serves 2 to 4

Grilled Pickerel in Foil

Getting tired of grilled fish? Well, here's a change. Wrap delicate fillets of pickerel, sole, turbot or catfish in foil with some flavorings and steam your fish on the grill. It cooks evenly and is always a great surprise when opened.

4	pickerel fillets (each 6 oz.)	1/4 cup	sour cream
3 tbsp.	Bay Seasoning (page 101)	2 tbsp.	lemon juice
1/2	seedless cucumber	1 tbsp.	lemon pepper
4 cloves	garlic, minced	1 tbsp.	chopped fresh dill
1	large sweet onion, sliced		Salt
1/4 cup	mayonnaise		

1. Trim the pickerel so each fillet is no more than 6 inches long. Rub the fish with the Bay Seasoning, pressing the seasoning into the flesh. Set aside.
2. Peel the cucumber, cut in half lengthwise and thinly slice. In a bowl, combine the cucumber, garlic, onion, mayonnaise, sour cream, lemon juice, lemon pepper and dill. Season to taste with salt.
3. Cut 4 sheets of foil 12 × 24 inches and fold each piece in half to make a 12-inch square. Place 1 fillet on one side of each piece of foil, leaving a good-sized margin at the edge. Top each fillet with the cucumber mixture. Fold over the foil and crimp the edges to seal well.
4. Preheat grill to medium-high.
5. Grill pouches for 8 to 10 minutes per side.
6. Transfer pouches to plates and carefully open at the table.

Serves 4

Grilled Salmon with Blackberry Ginger Compote

I first made this salmon dish for Gord Ash, the former manager of the Toronto Blue Jays. I poached the salmon in duck fat for a few minutes and then finished it on the grill. Gord and his guests loved it. I even think they licked their plates. What a party, but that's a whole other story.

6	Atlantic salmon fillets (each 6 oz.)		2 tsp.	toasted sesame seeds
3 tbsp.	Indonesian Cinnamon Rub (page 105)			Salt and pepper to taste
3	green onions, finely chopped			***Blackberry Ginger Compote***
1	lime, juiced		2 cups	fresh blackberries
1/4 cup	olive oil		1/2 cup	sugar
1/4 cup	honey		1/2 cup	water
1/4 cup	white wine		1/4 cup	amaretto
2 tbsp.	minced fresh ginger		1 tsp.	minced fresh ginger
1 tbsp.	chopped fresh mint			

1. Rub the salmon with the Cinnamon Rub, pressing the seasoning into the flesh. In a glass dish large enough to hold the salmon in one layer, whisk together the green onions, lime juice, olive oil, honey, wine, ginger, mint, sesame seeds, salt and pepper. Add the salmon, turning to coat. Cover and marinate for 30 minutes.
2. Meanwhile, prepare the compote. In a medium saucepan, combine the blackberries, sugar, water, amaretto and ginger. Bring to a boil, stirring occasionally. Reduce heat and simmer, stirring occasionally, until the berries burst and the sauce is thickened, 10 to 15 minutes. Remove from heat and keep warm.
3. Preheat grill to medium-high.
4. Remove salmon from marinade (reserving marinade for basting). Grill salmon, basting with marinade, until just cooked through, 5 to 8 minutes per side.
5. Serve immediately with the compote.

Serves 6

Cedar-Planked Salmon with Crab and Scallop Crust

Planking is probably my signature method. I have written a book on the subject (Sticks and Stones: The Art of Grilling on Plank, Vine and Stone) and I am always looking for different ways to plank that oh so famous salmon. This recipe was prepared for my show King of the Q, and let me tell you, getting fresh salmon in Jamaica was a difficult chore!

6	skinless Atlantic salmon fillets (each 10 to 12 oz.)		1 cup	shredded mozzarella cheese
1/4 cup	Bay Seasoning (page 101)		1/4 cup	BBQ sauce
			1 tbsp.	Bay Seasoning (page 101)
Crab and Scallop Crust			1 tbsp.	chopped fresh dill
			12	large sea scallops
1 bunch	green onions, chopped		Special equipment:	1 untreated red cedar plank (at least 12 x 10 x 1 inch), soaked in water at least 4 hours or overnight
1	large red onion, finely chopped			
3 cloves	garlic, minced			
1 1/2 cups	cooked crab or lobster meat			

1. Preheat grill to high.
2. Rub salmon all over with the Bay Seasoning, pressing the seasoning into the flesh. Place the salmon on the plank.
3. In a bowl, combine the green onions, red onion, garlic, crab meat, mozzarella, BBQ sauce, Bay Seasoning and dill. Top the salmon with this mixture, pressing it gently to make it adhere.
4. Using a sharp knife, slice each scallop into 4 or 5 rounds. Lay 6 to 8 scallop slices evenly over the crusted salmon.
5. Place the plank on the grill and close the lid. Grill until salmon is just cooked through and the scallops are golden, 12 to 15 minutes. Periodically check the plank; if it is burning, spray it with water and move it to a cooler part of the grill.
6. Serve salmon smoking on plank.

Serves 6

Nelson's Blood Smoked Salmon

In Newfoundland, salmon was often dipped in a dark rum before it was smoked. In my dad's village this rum was called Nelson's Blood, a dark syrupy rum with lots of flavor.

1 side	Atlantic salmon, boneless and skin on (4 to 6 lb.)	1/2 cup	sugar
2 tbsp.	Bone Dust BBQ Spice (page 99)	1/2 cup	dark rum, plus extra for brushing
2 cups	chopped fresh dill		Maple smoking chips or chunks
1/2 cup	salt		

1. Place the salmon skin side down on a cookie sheet with sides at least 1/2 inch high. Rub the salmon with Bone Dust BBQ Spice, pressing the seasoning into the flesh. Sprinkle evenly with the dill.
2. Stir together the salt and sugar. Sprinkle evenly over the salmon and pat firmly. Pour the rum over the salmon. Cover with plastic wrap. Place a 2- to 3-lb. weight on top of the salmon and refrigerate for 24 hours.
3. Prepare your smoker according to manufacturer's instructions to a temperature of 175°F. (See page 115.)
4. Rinse salmon under cold water and pat dry with paper towels. Place salmon on top rack and brush with a little rum. Add soaked smoking chips and close the lid. Smoke salmon until just cooked and still moist, 2 1/2 to 3 1/2 hours, replenishing smoking chips, coals and water as required.
5. Remove salmon from smoker and let cool completely. Thinly slice and serve with cream cheese and bagels or any way you wish.

Serves 12

Bacon-Wrapped Sea Bass Kebabs with a Grand Pineapple Syrup

Sea bass is a wonderfully delicate fish. I do not recommend undercooking this fish, as that tends to toughen it. I prefer to cook it just through, so it is tender and succulent. The bacon adds flavor and fat and helps to keep the fish moist.

2 lb.	skinless sea bass fillets (each 2 inches thick)	4 cloves	garlic, chopped
1 tbsp.	Bay Seasoning (page 101)	1/2 cup	corn syrup
16 slices	bacon, partially cooked and still flexible	1/4 cup	Grand Marnier
		1/4 cup	pineapple juice
		2 tbsp.	olive oil
Grand Pineapple Syrup		1 tbsp.	minced fresh ginger
2	green onions, finely chopped	1 tbsp.	chopped fresh cilantro
1	small Scotch bonnet pepper, seeded and finely chopped		Salt and pepper to taste

1. Soak 8 bamboo skewers (about 10 inches) in warm water for 30 minutes. (Or use metal skewers.)
2. Cut the sea bass into 2-inch chunks (you should have at least 16 chunks). Rub the sea bass with the Bay Seasoning.
3. Wrap a slice of bacon around each chunk and push 2 bamboo skewers through the bacon side, putting 4 chunks on each kebab.
4. To prepare the syrup, in a small bowl, whisk together the green onions, Scotch bonnet pepper, garlic, corn syrup, Grand Marnier, pineapple juice, olive oil, ginger, cilantro, salt and pepper.
5. Preheat grill to medium-high.
6. Grill kebabs, basting with the pineapple syrup and turning carefully, until the fish is just cooked through, 15 to 20 minutes.
7. Serve immediately with Tropical Coleslaw (page 19).

Serves 4

Planked Crab-Stuffed Rainbow Trout

Planked trout is wonderful. I first planked trout for my television show Cottage Country. *The trout was stuffed with lemon and sage. It was delicious, but this version, as Emeril would say, is "kicking it up a notch."*

4	rainbow trout (each 10 to 12 oz.), scales, bones and fins removed, head and tail intact	1½ cups	fresh lump crab meat
		½ cup	mayonnaise
	Salt and pepper	¼ cup	fresh bread crumbs
2 tbsp.	butter	2 tbsp.	chopped fresh dill
2	shallots, finely chopped	2 tbsp.	lemon juice
1 clove	garlic, minced	Special equipment:	2 untreated cedar planks (at least 10 x 8 x 1 inch), soaked in water for 4 to 6 hours
2	green onions, finely chopped		
1	leek, cleaned, cut in half lengthwise and thinly sliced		

1. Rinse trout inside and out and pat dry with paper towels. Using a sharp knife, make 3 incisions ½ an inch deep and 2 inches apart on each side of the trout. Season trout inside and out with salt and pepper.
2. Melt the butter in a medium frying pan over medium-high heat. Sauté the shallots, garlic, green onions and leek until tender, 3 to 4 minutes. Let cool slightly. In a bowl, combine the leek mixture, crab meat, mayonnaise, bread crumbs, dill and lemon juice. Season to taste with salt and freshly ground black pepper. Mix thoroughly.
3. Spoon the stuffing into the trout cavities. Secure with toothpicks.
4. Preheat grill to high.
5. Place soaked planks on the grill and close the lid. Let the planks heat for 3 to 4 minutes or until they start to crackle and smoke.
6. Carefully open the lid and place 2 trout on each plank. Close the lid and bake the trout until the fish is firm to the touch and easily flakes with a fork, 15 to 20 minutes. Periodically check the planks; if they are burning, spray with water and move them to a cooler part of the grill.
7. Serve trout immediately.

Serves 4

Butterflied Shrimp Three Ways

Here are three easy bastes for grilled butterflied shrimp. They're also great with salmon, scallops and any other of your favorite grilled dishes.

12	colossal shrimp (8 to 9 per lb.)	Salt and pepper

1. Peel shrimp, leaving the tails intact.
2. Using a sharp knife, cut lengthwise down the back of the shrimp about three-quarters of the way through. Rinse under cold water to remove the vein. Pat dry with paper towels. Run your fingers along the cut, pressing firmly to slightly flatten and butterfly the shrimp. Season to taste with salt and pepper.
3. Preheat grill to high.
4. Grill shrimp, basting with one of the three following basting sauces, until opaque and just cooked through, 3 to 4 minutes per side.

Serves 4

Super Garlic Butter Baste

1/2 lb.	butter	1 tbsp.	Bone Dust BBQ Spice (page 99)
12 cloves	garlic, minced		
2	lemons, zested and juiced	1 tbsp.	sugar
1/4 cup	chopped fresh chives	1 tbsp.	cracked black pepper
1/4 cup	white wine		Salt to taste

1. In a small saucepan, melt the butter over medium heat. Stir in the garlic, lemon juice and zest, chives, wine, Bone Dust BBQ Spice, sugar, pepper and salt. Slowly heat, stirring occasionally, for 5 to 10 minutes. Remove from heat and keep warm.

Makes about 2 cups

Tandoori Baste

Look for tandoori paste in specialty food stores and East Indian markets.

1/4 lb.	butter	1/4 cup	honey
6 cloves	garlic, minced	1 tbsp.	minced fresh ginger
1/4 cup	tandoori paste	1/2 cup	yogurt
1/4 cup	lime juice		

1. In a small saucepan, melt the butter over medium heat. Whisk in the garlic, tandoori paste, lime juice, honey and ginger. Slowly heat, whisking occasionally, for 5 to 10 minutes. Remove from heat and whisk in the yogurt. Let cool.

Makes about 2 cups

Orange Jalapeño Baste

1/2 lb.	butter	1 tbsp.	finely chopped fresh ginger
3	jalapeño peppers, seeded and finely diced	1 tbsp.	cracked black pepper
		1 tbsp.	chopped fresh cilantro
1/2 cup	orange juice		Salt to taste
1/2 cup	honey		

1. In a small saucepan, melt the butter over medium heat. Whisk in the jalapeños, orange juice, honey, ginger, black pepper and cilantro. Heat, whisking occasionally, for 10 minutes. Season with salt to taste. Remove from heat and keep warm.

Makes about 2 cups

Sugarcane-Skewered
Appleton Rum Jumbo Shrimp

After a day of filming in southern Jamaica, the crew and I stopped off at the Appleton Distillery. Here we found rows of sugarcane along with casks of rum. This recipe is inspired by that day.

2	pieces fresh sugarcane (12 inches long)	1 tbsp.	chopped fresh cilantro	
12	super-jumbo shrimp (5 to 10 per lb.), peeled and deveined		Salt and pepper to taste	
3 tbsp.	Bone Dust BBQ Spice (page 99)	**Rum Glaze**		
4	green onions, chopped	1/2 cup	brown sugar	
1 cup	Appleton rum	1/2 cup	Appleton rum	
1/4 cup	olive oil	1/4 cup	orange juice	
1/4 cup	orange juice	2 tsp.	cornstarch, dissolved in 1 tbsp. water	
		2 tbsp.	cold butter	

1. Peel the sugarcane and cut each piece lengthwise into 6 skewers. With a sharp knife, cut a point on one end of each skewer.
2. Thread 1 shrimp onto each skewer. Season shrimp with Bone Dust BBQ Spice.
3. In a glass dish large enough to hold the 12 skewers, whisk together the green onions, rum, oil, orange juice, cilantro, salt and pepper. Add skewers, turning to coat shrimp. Cover and marinate for 20 to 30 minutes.
4. Prepare the glaze by heating the sugar, rum and orange juice in a small saucepan over medium heat. Stir in the cornstarch mixture. Bring to a low boil, stirring, and remove from heat. Whisk in the cold butter until fully incorporated. Season to taste with salt and pepper.
5. Preheat grill to medium-high.
6. Grill shrimp, basting liberally with the glaze, until just cooked through, opaque and firm to the touch, 3 to 4 minutes per side.

Serves 4 to 6

Grilled Garlic-Beer-Buttered Lobster Tails

For this recipe I like to use Caribbean lobster tails, which tend to have more meat. On the beach one evening during our film shoot in Jamaica, I prepared these succulent lobster tails basted with garlic butter and beer for Pamela. Oh, was the evening delicious!

4	frozen Caribbean lobster tails (each 8 oz.)	1/4 lb.	butter
4 tsp.	Bay Seasoning (page 101)	2 tbsp.	lemon juice
8 cloves	garlic, minced	1 tbsp.	chopped fresh dill
1 cup	beer		Salt and pepper to taste

1. Partially thaw lobster tails. Using a sharp knife, cut down the center of the lobster tail three-quarters of the way through the meat. Spread the tail open to butterfly. Season lobster with the Bay Seasoning.
2. In a small saucepan, combine the garlic, beer, butter, lemon juice and dill. Slowly heat, stirring, until the butter is melted and the mixture is hot. Remove sauce from heat and season with salt and pepper.
3. Preheat grill to medium-high. Place a sheet of foil on the grill.
4. Brush the lobster tails with the sauce and place meat side up on the foil. Grill, basting with the sauce, until the meat is opaque and just cooked through, 6 to 7 minutes. Do not overcook the tails or they will be tough.
5. Serve tails with the remaining butter sauce for dipping.

Serves 2 to 4 with lots of champagne or ice-cold beer

Grilled Oysters Rockefeller

One of my chefs on the set of King of the Q, *Mike McColl, works at Rodney's Oyster House in Toronto. One day Mike prepared these tasty treats for me.*

1 lb.	fresh spinach		Dash	hot sauce
2 tbsp.	butter		Pinch	nutmeg
4 cloves	garlic, minced			Salt and pepper
3	small shallots, diced		1¹⁄₂ cups	fresh lump crab meat
1 cup	heavy cream		18	oysters
¹⁄₄ cup	grated Parmesan cheese		2 cups	shredded Swiss cheese
1 tbsp.	chopped fresh tarragon			Lemon juice, for drizzling

1. Blanch spinach briefly in a pot of boiling water. Refresh under cold running water. Drain well and cool. With your hands, squeeze out moisture. Chop the spinach.
2. Melt the butter in a medium frying pan over medium-high heat. Sauté the garlic and shallots until tender, 2 to 3 minutes. Stir in the cream. Bring to a boil and reduce cream by half. Whisk in the Parmesan cheese, tarragon, hot sauce, nutmeg, salt and pepper. Remove from heat. Stir in the spinach and crab meat.
3. To shuck the oysters, grip each oyster flat side up in a folded kitchen towel. Working over a bowl to catch the liquor, find a small opening between the shells near the hinge and pry open with an oyster knife. Carefully remove the top shell (discard it or use for decoration). Loosen the oyster from the shell by running the oyster knife underneath the body. Gently remove the oyster from the shell and place it on paper towels to drain. Set aside the bottom shells. Add the oyster liquor to the spinach sauce.
4. Place an oyster in each bottom shell. Top each oyster with a heaping tablespoon of the sauce. Sprinkle with Swiss cheese.
5. Preheat grill to medium-high.
6. Place oyster shells on a grill topper and place on grill. Close the lid and grill until the cheese is melted and bubbling, 10 to 12 minutes.
7. Transfer oysters to a serving platter, drizzle with a little lemon juice and serve.

Serves 6

Grilled Calamari with Balsamic Butter Sauce

Soaking calamari in buttermilk before grilling tenderizes the squid.

12	medium fresh or thawed frozen whole squid	
1 cup	buttermilk	
2 tbsp.	Malabar Pepper Rub (page 96)	
4 cloves	garlic, minced	
1/4 cup	olive oil	
1/4 cup	balsamic vinegar	
2 tbsp.	chopped fresh basil	

Balsamic Butter Sauce

5 tbsp.	butter
4 cloves	garlic, minced
4	shallots, diced
2 tbsp.	capers, drained
1/2 cup	balsamic vinegar
	Salt and pepper

1. Pull the mantle (body) from the tentacles. Remove and discard the hard transparent pen (backbone) and other inner matter from the body of the squid. Rinse under cold water and peel off the outer membrane.
2. Cut the eye section away from the tentacles and remove the hard bone (beak) from the center of the tentacles. Rinse under cold water and pat dry.
3. Using a sharp knife, score the body of the squid every 1/2 inch, cutting about two-thirds of the way into the flesh. Place body and tentacles in a glass dish and cover with buttermilk, turning to coat. Marinate, covered and refrigerated, for 4 hours.
4. Discard buttermilk and pat dry with paper towels. Season the squid inside and out with the Pepper Rub. In the glass dish, whisk together the garlic, oil, vinegar and basil. Add squid, turning to coat. Marinate for 20 minutes.
5. Meanwhile, prepare the sauce. Melt 2 tbsp. of the butter in a small saucepan over medium-high heat. Sauté the garlic, shallots and capers until tender, 2 to 3 minutes. Stir in the vinegar. Bring to a boil and reduce vinegar by half. Remove from heat and whisk in the remaining 3 tbsp. of butter, 1 tbsp. at a time, whisking until incorporated. Season to taste with salt and pepper. Set aside and keep warm.
6. Preheat grill to medium-high.
7. Drain the squid well. Grill squid until just cooked through, 3 to 4 minutes per side.
8. Transfer calamari to a platter and pour over balsamic butter sauce.

Serves 6

Grilled Jumbo Frogs' Legs

While vacationing on Marco Island in Florida I grilled up some tender tootsies of jumbo Florida frogs' legs. That was the first time I'd ever grilled frogs' legs. It was a fun experience, and hey, they do taste like chicken!

12 pairs	fresh or thawed frozen frogs' legs	4 cloves	garlic, minced
1/4 cup	Bay Seasoning (page 101)	3/4 cup	oyster sauce
1/4 cup + 2 tbsp.	chili-flavored soy sauce	1/4 cup	rice vinegar
		2 tbsp.	sake or rice wine
1/4 cup	vegetable oil	1 tbsp.	sesame seeds
2	green onions, minced	2 tsp.	cracked black peppercorns
		2 tsp.	sesame oil

1. Rub the frogs' legs with the Bay Seasoning, pressing the seasoning into the meat. Place legs in a glass dish. Whisk together 1/4 cup of the chili-flavored soy sauce and the oil. Pour over the legs. Cover and marinate for 30 to 45 minutes.
2. Meanwhile, prepare the sauce. In a bowl, whisk together the remaining 2 tbsp. of chili-flavored soy sauce, the green onions, garlic, oyster sauce, vinegar, sake, sesame seeds, pepper and sesame oil.
3. Preheat grill to medium-high.
4. Grill frogs' legs, basting with sauce, until meat is firm and opaque, 3 to 5 minutes per side.
5. Serve immediately.

Serves 4

Lovely Libations and Dazzling Desserts

Drinks

Desserts

Aloha Frozen Pineapple Margarita

Try this twist on the old lime favorite. Use a good tequila; I like golden tequila.

16	ice cubes		1 oz.	coconut-flavored rum
1 cup	pineapple juice			**Fresh pineapple wedges, for garnish**
4 oz.	tequila			
2 oz.	peach schnapps			

1. Coat the rims of 2 cocktail glasses with sugar and chill them.
2. In a blender, combine the ice, pineapple juice, tequila, schnapps and rum. Blend until the ice is crushed.
3. Pour into the glasses and garnish with a wedge of pineapple.

Serves 2

Amanoka Rum Punch

For the juice blend, use your choice of orange, guava, mango, passion fruit and pineapple.

1 cup	sugar		1 cup	fresh lime juice
2 cups	water			**Plenty of ice**
4 cups	fruit juice blend			**Pineapple wedges and orange slices, for garnish**
3 cups	dark rum			

1. In a medium saucepan, heat the sugar and water, stirring, until the sugar dissolves and the mixture is clear. Bring to a boil and remove from heat. Let cool completely.
2. In a pitcher, combine the sugar syrup, fruit juices, rum and lime juice. Stir well.
3. Fill 4 highball glasses with ice cubes. Pour in the punch. Garnish with pineapple wedges and orange slices.

Serves 4

Calico Float

The Calico Kitchen was a hamburger joint on the outskirts of my hometown, Paris, Ontario. I remember they had a pretty tasty burger. But what I remember most was cherry Coke floats that we would add a little cherry whisky to.

2	large scoops good vanilla ice cream	1 cup	heavy cream
4 oz.	cherry whisky	2	maraschino cherries, for garnish
2 cans	cherry Coke		

1. Put a scoop of ice cream in each of 2 milkshake glasses. Pour 2 oz. of cherry whisky into each glass and top with cherry Coke. Top each with a $1/2$ cup of cream and garnish with cherries.
2. Serve with parfait spoons and straws.

Serves 2

Chocolate Banana Rum Milkshakes (a.k.a. Dirty Banana)

Milkshakes are a fantastic drink, rich, thick and icy cold. A really good milkshake should be made with the richest ice cream. A really good milkshake should be so thick that it makes your eyes bulge. And a really good milkshake should be so cold that your brain freezes.

My favorite drink in Jamaica was the Dirty Banana. Some people make this with ice, but I much prefer it made with chocolate ice cream.

1	ripe banana	1 to 2 cups	milk
4 scoops	chocolate ice cream		Chocolate syrup, for drizzling
4 oz.	rum		
2 oz.	rum cream liqueur or Irish cream liqueur	1 cup	whipped cream
		2	maraschino cherries, for garnish

1. Put banana, ice cream, rum and rum cream liqueur in a blender. Blend briefly. Pour in milk a little at a time, pulsing until smooth and desired consistency.
2. Pour into 2 milkshake glasses. Drizzle with a little chocolate syrup. Top each with 1/2 cup of whipped cream and a maraschino cherry.
3. Serve with straws.

Serves 2

Iced Coffee Frappé

It seems that every day there is a new coffeehouse opening up someplace on some corner in some town, and they all seem to serve the same stuff. Café au lait, cappuccino, latte, espresso, half decaf, unsweetened, short, tall, grande, venti, blah, blah, blah. It is all so boring. So liven up your morning cup of joe with this decadent and loaded frappé. And if it's still not good enough for you, replace the ice with ice cream.

12 to 16	ice cubes		3 oz.	coffee liqueur
1/2 cup	heavy cream		1 oz.	amaretto
1/4 cup	condensed milk		1 cup	cold coffee
4 oz.	vodka		1/4 cup	chocolate shavings, for garnish

1. In a blender, combine the ice, cream, condensed milk, vodka, coffee liqueur and amaretto. Blend until smooth.
2. Divide the coffee among 4 milkshake glasses. Pour in equal amounts of the frappé. Garnish with chocolate shavings and serve with straws.

Serves 4

Grilled Bacon-Wrapped Bananas with Bourbon Honey Sauce

I know it sounds weird, but try it. The sweet and salt combination really works.
Try these with baby bananas wrapped in half a slice of bacon. Serve with smoked chocolate ice cream (page 225). It may seem a little nutty, but it really works, baby.

4 to 8 slices	bacon	**Pepper**
4	ripe but firm bananas	

1. Partially cook the bacon until most of the fat has been rendered but bacon is still flexible. Drain on paper towels and let cool.
2. Peel the bananas. Wrap each banana with 1 or 2 slices of bacon, starting at one end and coiling around the banana. Secure with toothpicks. Season with pepper.
3. Prepare Bourbon Honey Sauce (recipe follows).
4. Preheat grill to medium.
5. Grill bananas, turning occasionally, until the bacon is crisp and the bananas are lightly charred and heated through, 5 to 8 minutes. During the last few minutes, baste with Bourbon Honey Sauce.
6. Serve with ice cream and drizzled with sauce.

Serves 4

Bourbon Honey Sauce

1/2 cup	honey		2 tbsp.	water
1/2 cup	light corn syrup		1 sprig	fresh thyme
2 oz.	bourbon		Pinch	cracked black pepper

1. In a small saucepan, combine the honey, corn syrup, bourbon, water, thyme and pepper. Bring to a boil, stirring occasionally. Reduce heat to low and simmer for 5 minutes. Remove from heat and let cool slightly.

Makes about 1 1/4 cups

Grilled Fruit Kebabs with Butter Rum Sauce

Use firm-fleshed fruit for grilling. I tend to stay away from berries on the grill, although jumbo strawberries can be grilled without too much difficulty. Fruit does not take a long time on the grill; you really just need to warm the fruit, which brings out more of its natural sweetness.

1/2	pineapple	1/2 cup	Grand Marnier
1	small cantaloupe, peeled and seeded		Cracked black pepper to taste
4	ripe but firm kiwifruit, peeled	1 pint	fresh raspberries
2	peaches		Vanilla ice cream

1. Soak eight 10-inch bamboo skewers in warm water for 15 minutes. (Or use metal skewers.)
2. Cut the pineapple and cantaloupe into 1- to 2-inch chunks (at least 16 pieces from each). Put in a large bowl. Cut each kiwifruit into 4 wedges; add to bowl. Cut each peach into 8 wedges; add to bowl.
3. Pour over Grand Marnier and season with pepper. Gently toss. Marinate for 20 minutes.
4. Thread equal amounts of fruit onto skewers.
5. Prepare the Butter Rum Sauce (recipe follows).
6. Preheat grill to medium-high.
7. Grill kebabs, turning carefully, until lightly charred and heated through, 2 to 3 minutes per side. Brush each kebab with Butter Rum Sauce during the last minute of cooking.
8. Serve with ice cream and extra sauce.

Serves 4 to 8

Butter Rum Sauce

3/4 cup	brown sugar		2 oz.	spiced rum
3/4 cup	heavy cream		Pinch	nutmeg
1/4 lb.	butter		1/2 cup	golden raisins

1. In a medium saucepan over medium heat, bring brown sugar, cream, butter, rum and nutmeg to a boil, stirring constantly. Reduce heat to low, stir in raisins and simmer for 5 minutes.
2. Remove from heat and let cool for 5 minutes before using.

Makes about 2 cups

Coconut Fruit Salad

It is truly satisfying to be able to extract the meat from a fresh coconut. I learned a few new tricks on how to open coconuts from my friends in Jamaica. But to learn these tricks, you will have to watch my show King of the Q.

For a stunning presentation, cut dried coconuts in half and remove the meat, using the shell as your bowl.

2	ripe coconuts	2 oz.	coconut rum
1	ripe mango, peeled and cut into 1-inch chunks	1 oz.	amaretto
1	ripe papaya, peeled, seeded and cut into 1-inch chunks	1 cup	raspberries
		1 cup	blueberries
1 cup	sliced strawberries	1	star fruit, cut crosswise into 8 slices
1/4 cup	honey		Fresh mint sprigs, for garnish
1/4 cup	orange juice		

1. Crack the coconut shell by hitting it firmly with a hammer. It may take a few whacks but the shell should eventually crack. Break open shell and drain off any coconut water, saving it for the salad. Carefully remove meat from shell and cut meat into small pieces. You will need about 2 cups of coconut chunks.
2. In a bowl, combine the coconut chunks, reserved coconut water, mango, papaya, strawberries, honey, orange juice, coconut rum and amaretto; gently mix. Fold in the raspberries and blueberries.
3. Spoon salad into bowls or the coconut shells. Garnish with slices of star fruit and sprigs of fresh mint. Serve immediately.

Serves 4 to 6

Smoked Chocolate

Smoking chocolate is not a normal everyday-cooking thing to do. You need a lot of patience and a little bit of luck (you don't want the chocolate to melt). You will be cold-smoking the chocolate; it is necessary to maintain a low temperature, no higher than 135°F. You can use many types of smoking chips to add flavor to your chocolate; I like to use cracked whole pecans in the shell for a distinctive sweet, nutty flavor.

2 lb.	milk, dark or white chocolate bars (at least 1 inch thick)	24	pecans in the shell, cracked lightly and soaked in water for 30 minutes

1. Remove the top rack of your smoker and wrap it in foil. Place the chocolate on the wrapped rack.
2. Prepare your smoker according to manufacturer's instructions to a temperature of 135°F, using 12 to 15 charcoal briquettes. Fill the water tray with ice and a few cups of cold water. (This will help keep the temperature low and the smoke cool.) Note that when you initially place the hot coals in the smoker the temperature may go over 400 degrees. If this happens, remove lid and allow the charcoal to cool.
3. Place the rack with the chocolate in the highest position of the smoker and as far away from the heat source as possible. Close the lid. Add 4 or 5 pecans to the hot coals.
4. Smoke chocolate until it is soft but not starting to melt, 35 to 45 minutes. Watch it carefully. Add more pecans and water periodically, being careful to maintain the temperature. If it gets too hot, remove the cover to allow the heat to escape. Do not worry about losing the smoke, because it does not take much smoke to add flavor to chocolate.
5. Remove chocolate from grill and let cool completely. Store in plastic bags.

Peanut Butter Cupcakes with Smoked Chocolate Butter Frosting

Serve these babies with a scoop of ice cream or a cold glass of milk (or beer).

2 cups	all-purpose flour		1/2 cup	crunchy peanut butter
3 tsp.	baking powder		1/3 cup	butter
1/2 tsp.	salt		2	large eggs, beaten
3/4 cup	heavy cream		1/2 cup	raspberry jam
1 tsp.	vanilla			Smoked Chocolate Butter
1 1/2 cups	brown sugar			Frosting (recipe follows)

1. Preheat oven to 350°F. Line 2 muffin tins with paper liners.
2. Sift together the flour, baking powder and salt; set aside. Combine cream and vanilla; set aside.
3. In a large bowl, cream the sugar, peanut butter and butter until light and fluffy. Beat in eggs. Alternately beat in the flour mixture and the cream mixture.
4. Spoon batter into muffin tins. Swirl 1 tsp. of raspberry jam into each cupcake.
5. Bake both tins on the middle rack of the oven until a toothpick inserted in the center comes out clean, 20 to 25 minutes. Transfer cupcakes to a cooling rack and let cool completely.
6. Spread frosting evenly and thickly over the cupcakes.

Makes about 24 cupcakes

Smoked Chocolate Butter Frosting

4 tbsp.	butter, at room temperature	3 oz.	smoked chocolate (page 222)
2 cups	icing sugar	6 tbsp.	heavy cream
1/8 tsp.	salt	1 tsp.	vanilla

1. In a medium bowl, cream butter until soft. Stir in 1 1/2 cups of the icing sugar and the salt.
2. Melt the chocolate in a double boiler set over barely simmering water. Add the cream and stir until well blended.
3. Alternately stir chocolate and the remaining icing sugar into the frosting. Stir in vanilla. If the batter is too thick, stir in a little heavy cream.

Makes enough frosting for 2 dozen cupcakes

Smoked Chocolate Crème Fraîche Ice Cream

In all my years as a chef and all my years of eating tubs of ice cream I have never come across Smoked Chocolate Ice Cream. This is a fun recipe and delicious too. Carefully smoke your chocolate and then prepare this decadent ice cream recipe.

3 cups	heavy cream	12	large egg yolks
2 cups	half-and-half cream	1 cup	crème fraîche or sour cream
2	vanilla beans, split lengthwise	1/4 cup	lemon juice
1 1/2 cups	sugar	12 oz.	smoked chocolate pieces (page 222)

1. In a heavy saucepan, combine the heavy cream and half-and-half. Scrape out the seeds of the vanilla bean and add these, and the bean, to the pot. Slowly bring mixture to a boil. Remove from heat and let cool slightly.
2. In a large bowl, whisk together the sugar and egg yolks until thick and smooth. Whisking constantly, slowly pour the heated cream into the egg mixture.
3. Return custard to saucepan and cook over medium heat, stirring constantly with a wooden spoon, until the custard thickens and leaves a trail when a finger is drawn across the spoon, 8 to 10 minutes. Be careful not to boil the custard. Strain through a fine mesh strainer and keep warm.
4. Melt the chocolate in the top of a double boiler set over barely simmering water. Whisk the warm chocolate into the warm custard until fully incorporated. Let cool, then chill.
5. Prepare ice cream in an ice cream machine according to manufacturer's instructions. Transfer to a plastic container and freeze until needed.

Makes about 2 quarts

Index